P9-ARZ-892

FORTRESS • 31

ROME'S NORTHERN FRONTIER AD 70–235

Beyond Hadrian's Wall

NIC FIELDS

ILLUSTRATED BY DONATO SPEDALIERE

Series editors Marcus Cowper and Nikolai Bogdanovic

First published in 2005 by Osprey Publishing
Midland House, West Way, Botley, Oxford OX2 0PH, UK
443 Park Avenue South, New York, NY 10016, USA
E-mail: info@ospreypublishing.com

ISBN-13 : 978-1-84176-832-8
Cartography: Map Studio, Romsey, Hants
Design: Ken Vail Graphic Design, Cambridge, UK
Index by David Worthington
Originated by The Electronic Page Company, Cwmbran, UK
Printed and bound in China through Bookbuilders
Typeset in Monotype Gill Sans and ITC Stone Serif
08 09 10 11 12 13 12 11 10 9 8 7 6 5 4

A CIP catalogue record for this book is available from the British Library.

FOR A CATALOGUE OF ALL BOOKS PUBLISHED BY OSPREY MILITARY AND AVIATION
PLEASE CONTACT:

NORTH AMERICA
Osprey Direct, C/o Random House Distribution Centre, 400 Hahn Road,
Westminster, MD 21157
E-mail:info@ospreydirect.com

ALL OTHER REGIONS
Osprey Direct, The Book Service Ltd, Distribution Centre, Colchester Road,
Frating Green, Colchester, Essex, CO7 7DW
E-mail: customerservice@ospreypublishing.com

www.ospreypublishing.com

Artist's notes

Readers may care to note that the original paintings from which
the colour plates in this book were prepared are available for
private sale. All reproduction copyright whatsoever is retained by
the Publishers. All enquiries should be addressed to:

Sarah Sulemsohn
Tel-fax: +39 0575 692210
info@alinaillustrazioni.com
www.alinaillustrazioni.com

The Publishers regret that they can enter into no correspondence
on this matter.

Image credits

Unless otherwise indicated, the photographic images that appear
in this work are from the author's collection.

Measurements

Distances, ranges, and dimensions are given in metric. To covert
these figures to Imperial measures, the following conversion
formulae are provided:

1 millimetre (mm)	0.0394 in.
1 centimetre (cm)	0.3937 in.
1 metre (m)	1.0936 yards
1 kilometre (km)	0.6214 miles
1 gram (g)	0.0353 ounces
1 kilogram (kg)	2.2046 lb
1 tonne (t)	0.9842 long ton (UK)

The Fortress Study Group (FSG)

The object of the FSG is to advance the education of the public in
the study of all aspects of fortifications and their armaments,
especially works constructed to mount or resist artillery. The FSG
holds an annual conference in September over a long weekend
with visits and evening lectures, an annual tour abroad lasting
about eight days, and an annual Members' Day.
The FSG journal FORT is published annually, and its newsletter
Casemate is published three times a year. Membership is
international. For further details, please contact:
The Secretary, c/o 6 Lanark Place, London W9 1BS, UK

Contents

Introduction

The Roman 'period' in what is now Scotland was actually a series of distinct episodes. These varied in length from a single campaign to the absorption of lowland Scotland into the Roman Empire for a generation or two. Throughout this period the nature of the contact was essentially military, and no other country can boast so wide a range or so many examples of military installations, albeit built more often in timber and turf than in mortared stone, surviving anywhere in the empire. The aim of this brief work, therefore, is to explain these archaeological remains and place them in a broader historical context.

The Romans first heard of the Caledonii soon after Claudius invaded Britain in AD 43, but they did not advance into Scotland until some 35 years later, when Cn. Iulius Agricola was provincial governor (AD 77–84). Agricola was to spend six campaigning seasons in Scotland, the last culminating in the defeat of the Caledonii at the battle of Mons Graupius (AD 83). Although it appears that he established a 'frontier' along the Gask Ridge, as well as consolidating the Forth–Clyde line (the future site of the Antonine Wall), the occupation of lowland Scotland was to be fairly brief. Agricola was recalled in AD 84, and there was a withdrawal to the Tyne–Solway line (the future site of Hadrian's Wall).

The decision to abandon Hadrian's Wall and to advance the frontier (*limes*) of the province of Britannia more than 70 miles coincided with the accession of Antoninus Pius (AD 138), as well as the arrival of a new governor, Q. Lollius Urbicus (AD 139). By the time Lollius Urbicus had left Britannia (AD 143), the new *limes* across the Forth–Clyde isthmus had been built. The Antonine Wall, however, was to mark the northern frontier of the empire for little more than 20 years.

After Caledonian incursions from the north in AD 197, Septimius Severus (r. AD 193–211) arrived in AD 208, with his sons Caracalla and Geta, together with substantial military forces in order to restore order along the northern frontier, briefly reoccupying and repairing sections of the Antonine Wall. As such, Septimius Severus is identified as the architect of the Wall by the late fourth-century commentator Flavius Eutropius (*Breviarium ab urbe condita* 8.19.1).

An inscribed stone (*RIB* 1147) proving that Q. Lollius Urbicus was in Britannia as governor as early as AD 139, the year Antoninus Pius, as emperor, was consul for a second time. Found at Corbridge (Coria), where Dere Street crosses the Tyne, the inscription records the construction of buildings in the reoccupied fort by *legio II Augusta*. (Author's collection)

His [Septimius Severus'] final campaign was in Britannia, and so fortified with complete security the provinces he had recovered, he built a wall (*murus*) for 32 Roman miles from sea to sea.

The story, repeated by both Sex. Aurelius Victor (*Caesares* 20.4, cf. *Epitome* 20) and the *Scriptores Historiae Augustae* (Severus 18.2), was continued in the fifth century by writers like Paulus Orosius (*Histrorium adversus paganos* 7.17.8), though with the difference that the wall is now an earth rampart (*vallum*). These references, presumably to the Antonine Wall, were ultimately to find their way into the Venerable Bede (*Historia Ecclesiastica gentis Anglorum* 1.5), writing in Jarrow during the second quarter of the eighth century:

After fighting many great and hard battles, he [Septimius Severus] decided to separate the part of the island over which he had regained control, from the other uncon-quered tribes, not by a wall (*murus*) as some think, but by a rampart (*vallum*). For a wall is made of stones but a rampart, with which the forts are strengthened to resist the violence of the enemy, is made of sods cut from the earth and is raised high above the ground like a wall. In front is the ditch from which the sods have been lifted and above it are fixed stakes made of the strongest wood. So Severus constructed a great ditch from sea to sea and a very strong rampart fortified by numerous towers (*turres*) upon it.

The Antonine Wall ran from sea to sea across the 'wasp's waist' of Scotland and, apart from the reference to towers (which may be forts), the scholar-monk's description of the 'Severan Wall' fits it well.

Despite heavy casualties, mainly sustained in ambushes in difficult terrain, the Caledonii were suitably cowed and Septimius Severus took the honorific title *Britannicus*, 'conqueror of Britannia' (*SHA* Severus 18.2, *ILS* 431). After only a few years, though, the Antonine Wall was once more abandoned, this time permanently and the northern frontier reverted south once again to Hadrian's Wall. Readers are advised to consult the author's previous title in this series, Fortress 2: *Hadrian's Wall* AD *122–410*.

The erection of a temple to Mercury is recorded on this altar (*RIB* 2148) from Castlecary, Antonine Wall. Soldiers (*milites*) of *legio VI Victrix*, originating from Italy and Noricum, dedicated it. Mercury was the wing-footed messenger as well as the deity who watched over trade and commerce, and thievery. He was associated with peace and prosperity, and boundaries and frontiers. (Author's collection)

Agricola's northern campaigns

Apart from mentions by Dio (66.20.1-3), a lapidary inscription (*RIB* 229a) at Verulamium (St Albans), an inscribed lead water pipe (*RIB* 2434.1-2) from Deva Victrix (Chester), and a writing tablet (*Tab. Luguval.* 44) from Luguvalium (Carlisle) recording a trooper from *ala Gallorum Sebosiana* detached to his staff, Cn. Iulius Agricola is known entirely from the biography by his son-in-law Tacitus. It is a scrappy sort of treatise, which starts off as though intended to be a history of Britannia and the Britons, but then drifts into being a rather terse and over fulsome account of his father-in-law's term as governor. In the same year (AD 98) Tacitus published the *Germania*, which, as the title suggests, is a detailed study of the tribes of northern and central Europe. It contains no references to Britannia.

Born in the colony of Forum Iulii (Fréjus, Côte d'Azur) in Gallia Narbonensis, at the age of 37 Agricola was appointed governor (*legatus Augusti pro praetore*) of Britannia by Vespasian (AD 77). The emperor himself had served, with distinction, in the original expedition to the island under Claudius (Suetonius *Divus Vespasianus* 4.1). There was a particular factor in the choice of Agricola as governor of Britannia. He was a strong supporter of the Flavian dynasty, having gone over to Vespasian (March AD 69), as implied by Tacitus (*Agricola* 7.2), before the would-be emperor had even publicly declared his hand (July AD 69). He had also served in the province twice before, as a senior military tribune (*tribunus laticlavius*) during the Boudican revolt (AD 60–61) and as the legionary legate (*legatus legionis*) of *legio XX Valeria Victrix* (AD 70–73). Agricola, unusually for a Roman governor, came to the province with considerable local knowledge and experience.

It goes without saying that our knowledge of Agricola's tenure as governor is greatly enhanced by Tacitus' brief biography (or perhaps hagiography) of his father-in-law. Some care, however, should be taken when using the *Agricola* (*de vita Iulii Argicolae*) as a source since it is a laudatory biography written as an act of devotion (*pietas*). But the fact remains that much of what this vital source covers is probably true even if the credit need not be entirely accorded to Agricola.

The seven campaigning seasons of Agricola, as described by Tacitus, can be summarised as follows:

AD 77   Suppresses the revolt of the Ordovices and reoccupies Môn (Anglesey).

AD 78   In northern England among the Brigantes: measures to promote, as Tacitus stresses (*Agricola* 21), 'romanisation'.

AD 79   Advances to the Tay estuary (*Tanaus*) and builds forts ('glen-blocker' forts – possibly the Gask Ridge).

AD 80   Consolidates along the Forth–Clyde isthmus (*Clota et Bodotria*): Tacitus notes (*Agricola* 23) the isthmus was firmly held by garrisons (*praesidia*).

AD 81   Operates in the south-west of Scotland: Tacitus merely states Agricola advanced through 'repeated and successful battles' (*Agricola* 24.1).

AD 82   Tackles the Caledonii north of the Forth (Bodotria), a victory narrowly eluding him: *legio VIIII Hispana* badly mauled during a night attack upon its marching-camp.

AD 83   Finally shatters the resistance of the Caledonii at Mons Graupius.[1]

---

[1] Note the brief chronology for Agricola's governorship (after Hanson 1991: 40–45).

Bennachie, looking west from Chapel of Garioch, with Mither Tap (518m) prominent on the left. The bare granite outcrop of this most easterly of the Bennachie summits is surrounded by a vitrified Iron Age hill fort. Although not the highest point of the massif it is the most conspicuous. (Author's collection)

Bennachie, looking south-west from Mill of Carden, the possible location of the Roman left flank at Mons Graupius. Clearly visible is the outline of four peaks – Mither Tap, Oxen Craig, Watch Craig, and Hermit Seat (left to right) – along the east–west ridge of the mountain. (Author's collection)

His first action was the suppression of the Ordovices of what is now central and north Wales (AD 77). Agricola had arrived in the province late in the season and thus the following summer (AD 78) was his first full campaigning season. It is usually assumed that this season's campaign was in the territory of the Brigantes where, according to Tacitus (*Agricola* 20.3), he built forts – although some of this period might have been spent north of the Solway in what is now southern Scotland, as he also operated there during his third season (AD 79), ravaging tribes as far north as the estuary of the Tay. Again, according to Tacitus (*Agricola* 22.1) he built forts. The following year (AD 80) saw Agricola consolidating on the Forth–Clyde line with clearly no advances the next year either. There were, however, the campaigns north of the Forth against the Caledonii, his sixth (AD 82), when victory narrowly eluded him, and his seventh (AD 83), which culminated in Mons Graupius. Recalled in spring AD 84, he was denied further appointments because of, according to Tacitus (*Agricola* 41.4, cf. Dio 60.20.3), Domitian's malice and jealousy.

Consolidation along the Forth–Clyde

It was during Agricola's consolidation of lowland Scotland that the value of the Forth–Clyde isthmus as a boundary was first recognised. For once Tacitus' narrative (*Agricola* 23) is geographically precise:

[A] good place for halting the advance was found in Britannia itself. The Clyde and Forth (*Clota et Bodotria*), carried inland to a great depth on the tides of opposite seas, are separated by only a narrow neck of land. The isthmus was now firmly held by garrisons (*praesidia*), and the whole expanse of country to the south was safely in our hands.

Unfortunately, few sites can be positively attributed to Agricola. Since so many forts in Scotland have both Flavian and Antonine occupation, it is assumed that these first-century isthmus garrisons must lie beneath the later Antonine Wall. In no case, however, has this been proved by the discovery of any structural remains, though it seems a strong possibility at five sites (Old Kilpatrick, Balmuildy, Cadder, Castlecary and Mumrills) on the basis of the number and variety of first-century artefacts (glass, ceramics, bronze coins or *asses*) recovered there.

Mons Graupius

The climax of Tacitus' *Agricola* is the battle of Mons Graupius. There have been many attempts to locate the site of the battle, but all we really know is what Tacitus tells us and, suffice to say, none of his evidence is over-helpful. Nevertheless, the ubiquitous instrument of Roman mobility was the marching-camp, and those of Agricola that extend north and north-west in an arc from near Stonehaven to the pass of Grange just east of the Spey, are useful pointers. Several criteria can be used to identify those marching-camps most conceivably the work of Agricolan forces. They include a tendency to squareness of plan, and a method of gateway defence incorporating the *clavicula*, an extended arc of ditch and rampart that compelled an attacker to expose his right or unshielded side to the camp's defenders.

Assembled under the leadership of Calgacus (literally 'the Swordsman', cf. the Middle Irish word *colg*, 'sword'), 'the full force of all' the Caledonian tribes, 30,000 warriors, occupied the slopes of Mons Graupius (*Agricola* 29.3-4). The size of Agricola's army is not given, but Tacitus does say the enemy had a 'great superiority in numbers' (*Agricola* 35.4). Agricola certainly had 8,000 auxiliary infantry and probably 5,000 auxiliary cavalry together with *vexillationes* from the four legions (*II Adiutrix pia fidelis, II Augusta, VIIII Hispana, XX Valeria Victrix*) of Britannia (*Agricola* 35.2, 37.1), giving perhaps a total force of some 20,000 (St Joseph 1978: 283). Tacitus does name some of the auxiliary infantry units present on the day: four cohorts of Batavi, two cohorts of Tungri (*Agricola* 36.1), and an unspecified number of Britons recruited from the tribes in the south long since conquered (*Agricola* 29.2).

The identification of these units is not certain. Despite this, however, *cohortes I, III* and *VIIII Batavorum* are attested epigraphically in Britannia, *cohors VIIII* at the end of the first century as the garrison of the Stanegate fort at Vindolanda (*Tab. Vindol.* II 159, 282, 396, cf. III 574), with *cohors III* based somewhere in the vicinity (*Tab. Vindol.* II 263, 311), and *cohors I* early in the second century as the garrison of the Stanegate fort at Carvoran (*RIB* 1823–24). Likewise, *cohortes I* and *II Tungrorum milliariae*, the latter part-mounted (*equitata*), also formed part of the permanent military presence in Britannia, *cohors I* being the earliest attested garrison at Vindolanda (*Tab. Vindol.* II 154), leaving there soon after AD 90 to be replaced by *cohors VIIII Batavorum*. Like its sister unit, *cohors II* still formed part of the garrison of Britannia in the third century, the cohort being last attested in AD 241 at Castlesteads on Hadrian's Wall (*RIB* 1983, cf. *ND* XL$_{40}$). The Britons may have been present in their

Altar (*RIB* 2092) dedicated to *Disciplina Augusti* by *cohors II Tungrorum milliaria equitata coram laudata*, the garrison at Birrens (Blatobulgium) during the Antonine period. The cult links two concepts, namely obedience to the emperor and military efficiency. The top of the altar is hollowed out to form a focus where offerings such as fruit, grain or wine could be deposited. (Author's collection)

Whereas the Antonine Wall rampart has suffered badly from intensive farming and urban development, the ditch is a more formidable obstacle to progress, and often survives impressively in places where the rampart has completely disappeared. One such example is the substantial portion of ditch visible in Callendar Park, here some 1.8m deep and traceable for 500m. (Author's collection)

own ethnic cohort, a *cohors Brittonum*, for such are attested serving overseas during the reign of Trajan. For instance, a military diploma of AD 110 names M. Ulpius Longinus, Belgus, of *cohors I Brittonum* (*CIL* 16.163, cf. 160). The adjectival form *Belgus*, 'from the *civitas Belgarum*', identifies this discharged veteran as hailing from the canton of the Belgae in central southern Britannia. Longinus had completed at least 25 years' service in AD 110, and so had enlisted in AD 85 at the latest. The first cohorts of *Brittones* to be mentioned are those in the army of Vitellius, governor of Germania Inferior and emperor-to-be, which fought at Bedriacum in AD 69 (Tacitus *Historiae* 1.70).

Agricola deployed the auxiliary cohorts in the centre, with their ranks opened out, and 3,000 auxiliary cavalry on the wings, which probably comprised six *alae quingenariae*. A further four *alae quingenariae*, some 2,000 troopers, were kept in reserve. The legionary *vexillationes* were to the rear, drawn up in front of the marching-camp. The Caledonii were deployed in closed-packed tiers on the gentle slope with its van on the level ground.

The Caledonian war-chariots raced across the ground between the two armies, only to be routed by the auxiliary cavalry. Next came a brisk exchange of missiles followed by the Roman advance up the slope. 'Striking them with the bosses of their shields, and stabbing them in the face' (*Agricola* 36.2), the auxiliary infantry were initially successful and were soon joined by the auxiliary cavalry. The sheer numbers of the Caledonii, however, combined with the roughness of the terrain, halted this advance and gradually the auxiliary cohorts began to be outflanked. In a counter-move Agricola sent in his reserve *alae*, which stemmed the flanking movement and then, in turn, fell on the rear of the war-bands, which accordingly broke. The legionaries, the citizen-soldiers of Rome, had not been engaged. This was an achievement that occasioned one of Tacitus' characteristic epigrams: 'a great victory glorious for costing no Roman blood' (*Agricola* 35.2).

The exact location of the battle is unknown, but below the Iron Age hillfort of Mither Tap o' Bennachie (pronounced Ben-a-Hee), the most north-easterly mountain in Aberdeenshire and on the border between the Highlands and the Lowlands, has been suggested as a possible site. At Logie Durno near Pitcaple, 6 miles (9.6km) north-west of Inverurie, is a Roman marching-camp of some 144 acres (*c*. 58.25 ha). Unfortunately the camp, the largest known beyond the Forth and big enough to accommodate Agricola's entire force with room to spare, is undated. However, a persuasive case was made out by J.K.S. St Joseph (1978) for identifying it as Agricola's base on the eve of the battle, which (it has been suggested) was fought out on the lower slopes of Bennachie, 3 miles (4.8km) to the south-west. Bennachie (528m) is an isolated granite massif that dominates the surrounding plain and, with its outline of four peaks (Mither Tap, Oxen Craig, Watch Craig, and Hermit Seat) along an east-west ridge, is visible from the outskirts of Aberdeen 16 miles (25.6km) away.

Marching-camps

A Roman army on the march habitually defended itself when it rested for the night by erecting a marching-camp (Josephus *Bellum Iudaicum* 3.76, Vegetius 1.21, cf. 4), the equivalent of 'digging-in' for a modern infantryman. It was an instrument of aggression as much as of defence and it played an essential part, at least down to the third century, in Roman military thinking. It was specifically designed for operations deep in hostile territory and had three important functions. Firstly, and primarily, if offered a secure base from which to continue the advance or, more specifically, the thrust towards conquest. Secondly, it provided defence upon which to retire in the event of receiving a check in the field. Thirdly, the daily construction of the marching-camps left in the wake of the army a series of fortified stepping-stones by means of which the advance could be sustained. Clausewitz indirectly gives support to the technique when he praises Napoleon, who 'always took great care with these measures for the protection of the rear of his army and, therefore, in his most audacious operations, risked less than was usually apparent' (*Principles of War* 3.3.3).

Aerial reconnaissance makes clear that their plans are often irregular, 'as required by the terrain' (Vegetius 3.8, cf. Polybios 6.27.1). They consist of an earth rampart (*agger*), with some form of timber obstacle. The examples of the square-section wooden stakes (*pila muralia*) for this that have survived are sharpened at both ends, and have a narrower 'waist' in the middle for tying together. They cannot, therefore, have been set vertically in the rampart, as hammering them in would have damaged the sharp ends. It seems more likely that the sets of three or four were lashed together with pliable withies or leather ties at angles and placed on the rampart crown as giant 'caltrops' – what Vegetius (3.8) calls *tribuli* – and each of these would also no doubt have been tied with its neighbour. Although this was never considered a defensive structure, tangling with such an obstacle in an attack would have caused chaos. Each legionary carried two *pila muralia*, preferably in oak, as part of his regulation marching order.

A general view of the suggested site of Mons Graupius as seen from Maiden Castle, on the lower, north-eastern slopes of Bennachie, looking north towards Mill of Carden. If indeed this is the battlefield, then the Caledonian right flank was presumably positioned here. (Author's collection)

Outside the defences was a single V-shaped ditch (*fossa*), usually not more than a metre deep and across, the spoil (or upcast) from which went to form the rampart. The entrances of marching-camps (there were no gateways as such) were of two types. First, those defended by *tituli*, which were short stretches of rampart and ditch set a few metres in front of the gap in the main rampart spanning its width. In theory they would break the charge of an enemy. Second, those defended by *claviculae*, which were curved extensions of the rampart (and sometimes its ditch), usually inside the area of the camp, although external and double *claviculae* are also known. They would force an oblique approach towards the entranceway, usually so that an attacker's sword arm faced the rampart, denying him the protection of his shield.

Within the camp the tent-lines were deliberately laid out, each line in its customary space so that every unit knew exactly where to pitch its tents. According to Hyginus Gromaticus (*De munitionibus castrorum* 1, cf. Vegetius 2.13) each tent (*papilio*) measured, exclusive of guy-ropes, 10 Roman feet (2.96m) square and housed eight men (*contubernium*) and their equipment. They were made of best-quality leather – pieces from Newstead and Birdoswald have been identified as calf – with access back and front and enough headroom inside to enable a man to stand up. Made of 25 shaped panels, which were sewn together, they could be rolled up into a long sausage-shape and in this form were carried by mule. This shape may have given rise to the nickname *papilio* (literally 'butterfly') as it rolled up like a grub, and its wings probably reminded the soldiers of the insect emerging from the chrysalis.

Between the rampart and the tent-lines was a wide open area known as the *intervallum*, which ensured all tents were out of range of missiles thrown or shot from outside the camp. More importantly, this space allowed the army to form itself up ready to deploy into battle order. Calculating the number of troops each marching-camp would have housed is fraught with difficulties. As a rule of thumb, however, it is usually thought that a full legion (5,120 men all ranks) could be accommodated under leather in about 30 acres (12 ha), compared with 50–60 acres (20–25 ha) for a permanent legionary fortress. The *intervallum* also allowed full access to the defences.

The marching-camp offered protection against surprise attack. Normally the rampart and ditch were sufficient only to delay attackers, not to stop them. The Romans rarely, if ever, planned to fight from inside the camp, preferring to advance and meet the enemy in the open. However, this was not always the

Cramond Kirk, which sits upon the site of the *principia* of the Roman fort, is a powerful symbol of continuity. It is no coincidence that the present church, on the site of its medieval predecessors, directly overlies the *principia*, the most substantial building in the fort and the focus of cultic activity for the garrison. (Esther Carré)

Rough Castle was the second smallest fort on the Antonine Wall, occupying only about 0.4 ha, but the earth rampart and ditches are very well preserved on all three sides. The double ditches defending the fort's west side, and the causeway that crosses them from the west gateway (*porta principalis sinistra*), are shown here. (Author's collection)

Forts on the Antonine Wall often had annexes attached to them, by which we mean enclosures defended by a rampart and ditch. Where excavated they have been found to contain hearths and ovens, and industrial workshops, as well as cultic shrines and sometimes the fort bathhouse. This is certainly the situation at Rough Castle. (Author's collection)

case. Describing the build-up to Agricola's sixth campaign (AD 82) Tacitus says (*Agricola* 25.3):

> The Caledonii got ready to fight with great preparation of equipment, all of which was exaggerated by rumour, as usually happens when real information is in short supply. They even launched attacks on some forts and, by taking the offensive, increased the feeling of panic.

One such attack was the one launched, at night, upon the marching-camp of *legio VIIII Hispana*. Having slain the camp sentries the Caledonii, in the dramatic words of Tacitus, 'burst in, amidst scenes of panic and sleep-befuddled confusion' (*Agricola* 26.1).

Military roads

A road system not only allowed for adequate movement of men and *matériel*, it also greatly eased the passage of information, that is, the reports, returns, and requisitions upon which the Roman army depended for its very existence. It has been estimated (Maxwell 1998: 29) that the Agricolan conquest required more than 400 Roman miles (*c*. 590km) of road to be constructed in northern Britannia.

Although the basic principles are constant throughout the empire, local conditions, including the availability of suitable construction materials and the time available to complete the job, dictate the details of road construction. In Scotland a wide variety of construction techniques was used, reflecting the changing character of the terrain through which the roads ran. In areas with well-drained and firm subsoil little effort would be made to provide boulder bottoming – only enough to ensure the correct cambered profile. On softer ground, such as peat bog, the road builders either excavated down to bedrock, or 'floated' the road mound on a raft of sand or gravel.

The road usually took the form of a bed, or *agger*, raised above the level of the surrounding land, with drainage ditches on either side. Formed of the material thrown up from the road side-ditches, the bed was cambered for drainage and could be 10m or more in width. It was rarely less than about 4m in width, so as to allow room for two, wheeled vehicles to pass. In Scotland two-thirds of the road system was built to a standard carriageway width of 20 Roman feet (5.92m), but what could be termed as the central spine of the system, Dere Street, exhibits a more generous standard, perhaps as wide as 25–30 Roman feet (7.4–8.88m).

The road itself was built up in a series of layers, comprising a foundation of larger rocks, followed by smaller stones, gravel and sand laid down successively and pressed firmly into place. A cobbled surface was commonplace in towns or areas of heavy use, but often it was just firmly compacted gravel. Most of the material for bottoming and metalling came from roughly circular or oblong quarry-pits flanking the road and lying 5–15m from it. A strip of land was cleared to either side to provide visibility and protect travellers from sudden attack. Distances along the road were marked by milestones, of which only one has survived from Scotland – at Ingliston near Edinburgh, erected in the reign of Antoninus Pius (*RIB* 2313).

Statius (*Silvae* 4.3.40–55), in praising the Via Domitiana, a shortcut along the Via Appia, offers a very general and poetical sketch of marking out the road, excavating the ground, and filling in other material for the pavement or other surface layer:

One way to spot Roman roads today is by recognition of their cambered mounds across the landscape. Here we see the *agger* of the Military Way at Seabegs Wood, with the appearance of the drainage ditches being very subtle. This road provided a lateral communications link for the garrisons of the various Antonine Wall forts. (Author's collection)

> The first task here is to trace furrows, ripping up the maze of paths, and then excavate a deep trench in the ground. The second comprises refilling the trench with other material to make a foundation for the road build-up. The ground must not give way nor must bedrock or base be at all unreliable when the paving stones are trodden. Next the road metalling is held in place on both sides by kerbing and numerous wedges. How numerous the squads working together! Some are cutting down woodland and clearing the higher ground, others are using tools to smooth outcrops of rock and plane great beams. There are those binding stones and consolidating the material with burnt lime and volcanic tufa. Others again are working hard to dry up hollows that keep filling with water or are diverting the smaller streams.

All legionaries, as shown on Trajan's Column (scenes XXIII, XCII), were trained and equipped to construct roads, but labour for maintaining them was usually provided by the local population of the *civitas* or tribal canton through which a particular section ran. Typically 3–8m across and originally about 1.3m deep, the quarry-pits flanking the road system in Scotland are so numerous in places that they overlap, suggesting that later road-repair gangs may have dug some.

Case study 1: the *Auxilia*

As part of Augustus' military reforms, the auxiliary units (*auxilia*) of the Roman army were completely reorganised and given regular status. Trained to the same high standards of discipline as the legions, the men were long-service professional soldiers like the legionaries and served in units that were equally permanent. Drawn from a wide range of warlike peoples throughout the provinces, especially on the fringes of the empire, the *auxilia* were non-citizens and would receive Roman citizenship on completion of their service, which lasted 25 years. The senior officers and commanders, on the other hand, were Roman citizens (i.e. the decurions, centurions, prefects and tribunes).

The *auxilia* were a cheaper and, given their primary organisation at a lower level (i.e. *cohortes* for infantry and *alae* for cavalry), more flexible way of providing the army with the manpower to fulfil its role, especially along the frontiers of the empire. To the *auxilia* fell the tasks of patrolling, containing raids, tax collecting, and the multitudinous duties of frontier troops – the legions were stationed within the frontiers, both to act as a strategic reserve and to intimidate potentially rebellious indigenous 'friendlies'. In particular, the mixed cohorts (*cohortes equitatae*), which included both foot and horse in a ratio of about four to one, were especially suited to garrison and local policing activities.

At full strength, the cohort (*cohors*) was either of 480 men (6 centuries) or 800 men (10 centuries). The smaller cohort was called *quingenaria* (nominally 500) and the larger *milliaria* (nominally 1,000). A cohort could be part mounted (*equitata*). The cavalry *alae* were divided into 16 (*ala quingenaria*) or 24 (*ala milliaria*) *turmae*, each commanded by decurions (*decuriones*). At full strength a *turma* had 32 men so the *ala quingenaria* had 512 men, and the *ala milliaria* 768 men. The *cohors milliaria* was commanded by a tribune (*tribunus cohortis*), and the *cohors quingenaria* and all *alae* by a prefect (*praefectus cohortis*). It was not uncommon, however, for a legionary centurion (*centurio legionis*) to have command of an auxiliary cohort.

Infantry

Although there were specialist units of archers and slingers, it would be wrong to view the typical foot soldier of the *auxilia* as some form of light infantry. Weighed down with helmet, mail body-armour (*lorica hamata*), short sword (*gladius*), dagger (*pugio*), spear (*hasta*) and flat shield (*clipeus*), this equipment is not that of a nimble skirmisher. Auxiliaries formed the first line at Idistaviso (AD

The *via principalis* running between the two side gateways (*portae principales*) and the one (*via praetoria*) running from the main gateway (*porta praetoria*) form the typical T-shaped plan of a fort's interior. At their junction stands the *principia*. This photograph shows the *via principalis* of Cramond fort, with the *principia* (now occupied by the Kirk) to its left. (Esther Carré)

16) and Vetera (AD 70), operated in close-order using the traditional sword-fighting techniques of the Roman army at Mons Graupius (AD 83) and could even stand up to and beat legionaries as the Batavi rebels did in AD 70 (Tacitus *Annales* 2.16, *Agricola* 36.2, *Historiae* 4.20, 5.16). The essentially similar fighting techniques of the legions and the infantry of the *auxilia*, that is to come to close-quarters and to use both shield and sword offensively, emphasised the degree to which the latter became an essential and very efficient part of the Roman army. That these tactics were the practice of the period is amply shown on Trajan's Column where at least three scenes of battle depict auxiliaries in action and legionaries in reserve (e.g. scenes XXIV, LXVI, LXXII).

Cavalry

Drawn from peoples nurtured in the saddle, the cavalry of the *auxilia* provided a fighting arm in which the Romans were not so adept. As regards recruitment, Gauls, Germans, Celtiberians and Thracians were preferred. As is apparent from

'Block B' (buildings B1, B2, B3) at Cramond fort sits in the east *praetentura*, immediately north of the *via principalis*. In its final phase it served as a workshop (*fabrica*), the fort having been refurbished as a supply base in preparation for Septimius Severus' campaigns against the Caledonii. (Esther Carré)

The Antonine Wall ditch at Watling Lodge, looking west. Here it presents the visitor with a formidable barrier, preserving almost its original dimensions of 12.2m in breadth and 4.5m in depth. Like most military ditches, it is V-shaped in profile, the scarp and counter-scarp sloping up at an angle of 30 degrees to the vertical. (Author's collection)

Table 1: Recruitment of cavalry troopers (after Hyland 1990: 77)		
Province	**Number**	**Percentage**
Gallia Lugdunensis	13,000	33
Tarraconensis	6,000	15
Thracia	4,500	11.5
Pannonia	4,000	10
Gallia Belgica	3,500	9
Syria-Phoenice	2,000	5
Africa	2,000	5
Britannia	1,500	4
Syria-Palestina	1,000	2.5
Moesia	1,000	2.5
Gallia Narbonensis	1,000	2.5

the approximated figures in Table 1, which are representative of the period around AD 70, the three Gallic provinces provided some 44.5 per cent of the troopers serving in the auxiliary *alae*. Organised, disciplined and well trained, it was able both to skirmish and perform shock action. Cavalry, therefore, were useful in reconnaissance, communication and policing duties, as well as in battle. As part of the garrison of the Antonine Wall, perhaps their most crucial role came in the former.

Case study 2: the Caledonii

Claudius Ptolemaeus' list of the tribes of Britannia, written towards the middle of the second century but based on sources from the end of the previous century, records the Caledonii as a single tribe occupying the Highland massif (*Geographia* 2.3.8-12). On the other hand, Tacitus (*Agricola* 10.3, 25.3, 27.1, 31.4), and no doubt primarily his father-in-law, and Dio (77.12.1), to denote the lands and the people north of the Forth or Tay, use the name in a looser, collective sense. It is the latter definition that is followed here.

War-chariot
This was a single-axled vehicle, drawn by two ponies via a yoke-pole and traces, and carrying a charioteer and a warrior. C. Iulius Caesar (*Bellum Gallicum* 4.24, 33, 5.16–17), who faced war-chariots in southern Britannia, is quite specific in describing them as a means of transport to enable the warrior speedily to approach or retire from an engagement, which was fought on foot. Yet his praise for their skill in manoeuvring the chariots at high speed, including the ability to walk along the yoke pole, and his reference to the hurling of missiles from chariots on the move, implies a method of operating not unlike that of the cavalry. Caesar (*Bellum Gallicum* 5.19) claims that the Gallo-Belgic forces of Cassivellaunus, even when most had been disbanded still included 4,000 chariots. In all probability, however, war-chariots are unlikely to have been numerous since they will have represented the warrior aristocracy.

In his narrative dealing with Mons Graupius (AD 83), Tacitus (*Agricola* 35.3) merely says the Caledonian war-chariots noisily manoeuvred between the battle lines, launching a dense volley of javelins before being pushed aside by the auxiliary cavalry. Intriguingly, however, Tacitus says of the chariot crew that 'the charioteer has the place of honour, the combatants are mere retainers' (*Agricola* 12.1). It is possible that the Caledonii employed tactics different from those that Caesar had encountered in the south of the island some 130 years before (*Bellum Gallicum* 4.33). Prior to the decisive clash at Mons Graupius, Tacitus does say the

'the flat space between the two armies was taken up by the noisy manoeuvring of the charioteers' (*Agricola* 35.3). Whatever, the Caledonii were still employing chariots as a tactical weapon during the northern campaigns of Septimius Severus (AD 208–210). The contemporary historian Dio reports that they went into battle in chariots drawn by 'small, swift horses' (77.12.3), in other words ponies. Today we see their descendants in the heavier, taller British native ponies such as Fell, Dale, and further north the Highland (or Garron).

Archaeological evidence demonstrates that these chariots were small, very light and easily dismantled, their construction exhibiting a standard of carpentry that was extremely high, and equal to anything the Classical world could produce. For instance, a wheel discovered at the fort of Newstead, near Melrose, is constructed of three different types of wood: ash (one-piece felloe), willow (11 spokes), and elm (hub). Also, recent work on the Celtic chariot has re-evaluated its construction. Suspended from the double loops of heat-bent wood, which made up the sides of the vehicle, were leather thongs. These were attached to the floor of the cab, which was of interlaced leather straps. The whole thus acted as a form of suspension, thereby optimising the speed and manoeuvrability of the war-chariot.

War-band

It is likely that the boldest (or more foolhardy) and best equipped naturally gravitated to the front rank. Body-armour seems to have been very rare and the combination of shield, long slashing-sword, and spear(s) formed the equipment of most warriors. The appearance of the individual (body art, slaked hair, torque), his size, expressions and war cries, added to the din of clashing weapons and the carnyx, or war-horn, were clearly intended to intimidate the enemy before actually reaching them. In the words of Dionysios of Halikarnassos (*fl.* 30 BC) the enemy were 'threatened by shouting, singing, and by brandishing and clashing of arms' (14.9.4). If the enemy were persuaded that he was going to lose before an actual mêlée began, then a Caledonian charge would drive all before it. Tactics were simple and relied on a headlong charge, preferably downhill, by an obstreperous mass of warriors lead by their war leaders. As was common in all Celtic tribal-armies, the warriors were poorly disciplined and lacked training above the level of the individual. The charge, the centrepiece of Celtic offensive tactics, succeeded because of the emphasis on individual effort, but if the attack failed, it became clear that the Celts lacked the essential skills of military organisation.

At Mons Graupius, Tacitus clearly states (*Agricola* 36.1, 2) that the Caledonii were armed with small shields and long swords without points (i.e. the forged iron slashing-sword common to all Celts), which did not allow them the luxury of fighting in a confined space nor in close-order. Dionysios of Halikarnassos describes how Celtic warriors would raise their swords aloft and smote by throwing the whole weight of their bodies into the blow 'like hewers of wood' (14.10.1). Contrary to oft-quoted opinion of our Graeco-Roman authors, archaeological evidence shows that some Celtic sword-smiths were producing weapons of a very high quality. Indeed, few surviving blades descend to the inferior quality described by Polybios, who says (2.33.3):

They are effective only at the first blow. Thereafter their edges are immediately blunted and the blades become so bent lengthways and sideways that unless the men are given time to straighten them with the foot against the ground, the second blow has virtually no effect.

Polybios' story of the swords that bent reads like one of those tales told by soldiers to while away idle moments around the campfire. Nevertheless, other authors took up Polybios' comments and criticisms (Plutarch *Camillus* 41.4, Polyainos 8.7.2). The one notable exception is Philon of Byzantium (*fl. c.* 200

BC) who, in an illuminating passage written around the time of Polybios' birth, describes (*Belopeika* 4.71) how the Celts test the excellence of their swords:

> They grasp the hilt in the right hand and the end of the blade in the left: then, laying it horizontally on their heads, they pull down at each end until they [i.e. the ends] touch their shoulders. Next, they let go sharply, removing both hands. When released, it straightens itself out again and so resumes its original shape, without retaining a suspicion of a bend. Though they repeat this frequently, the swords remain straight.

Ironically, Polybios (3.49.11) later contradicts himself when he relates how Hannibal organised an extensive replacement of the worn and damaged weapons of his troops with Celtic ones, which does suggest Celtic arms were of good quality. Dio (77.12.3), recording the details of Septimius Severus' campaigns against the Caledonii, fails to mention their swords. However, what he does say is noteworthy, for their warriors were armed with a shield, dagger and short spear, the latter having a bronze 'door-knob' attached to the end of the shaft, which allowed the warrior to clash it against his shield and thus terrify the enemy. He also adds that they were very swift in running and very firm in standing their ground. Herodian (3.14.8), on the other hand, does refer to the Caledonii being armed with the sword, as well as a narrow, rectangular shield and a spear. A finely preserved example of such a shield, of alder with an oak handle and leather facing, was found at Clonoura, County Tipperary, and they are depicted in the left-hand relief of the distance slab (No. 1) from Bridgeness on the east terminus of the Antonine Wall.

Appearance

To the Graeco-Romans, the Celts per se were striking in demeanour because of their great height, blond or reddish hair, shaggy appearance and pale complexions. Descriptions of lime-washed hair combed into stiff spikes specifically refer to the Gauls (Diodoros 5.28.2), but it is reasonable to suggest that the Caledonii may have also treated their hair in this way. It should be noted the use of lime had a secondary affect, that is to say it also bleached the hair. The Celts themselves took great pride in their appearance, to impress each other and to alarm their foes on the field of battle. Tacitus (*Agricola* 11.2) considers red hair and large limbs as the defining mark of the Caledonii.

Both Dio (77.12.2) and Herodian (3.14.7) say the Caledonii went stark-naked and barefooted, and there are many references to the Celtic habit of fighting unclothed (Polybios 2.28.8, 30.1, 3.114.4, Diodoros 5.29.2, 30.3, Livy 38.21.9, 26.7). Elsewhere these sources also refer to the Celts as being naked only from the waist up (Polybios 2.28.7, Livy 22.46.6). Herodian reasons that the Caledonii did not wish to cover up the artwork on their bodies, having tattooed them with 'various designs and pictures of all kinds of animals' (3.14.7). The late fourth-century court poet Claudian (22.248, cf. 26.417) also mentions tattooing (*ferro picta*, literally 'iron-marked'), as does Jordanes (*fl.* AD 550), who claims the Caledonii had 'iron-painted bodies' (*Getica* 2.14).

Although no Briton's skin has ever been found tattooed, we do have Caesar's remarks about the painted bodies of the Britons. Clearly fascinated, he says 'all Britons dye their bodies with *vitrum*, which produces a bluish colour and gives them a wild appearance in battle' (*Bellum Gallicum* 5.14). The verb Caesar uses for the process is *inficere*, to stain or dye as oppose to puncturing, and his account gains credence from the recent discovery of clay-based copper pigment in the skin of the Lindow Man III, the second male body found in 1987. Pomponius Mela (*fl.* AD 43) also describes painted Britons and, like Caesar, calls the pigment *vitrum* or 'glass, crystal' (3.6.51). This is not the vegetable dye woad (*isatis tinctoria*), albeit known and used by the Britons and called *glastum* by Pliny (*Naturalis historia* 22.2), but a mineral-based pigment, such as malachite, which produces a blue-green paint for body marking. Caesar may have provided the inspiration for Augustan poetic allusions to painted Britons, one by Propertius and the other by Ovid. Whereas Propertius merely refers to 'the painted Briton' (2.18 b1, cf. Martial 11.53.1), Ovid speaks of *vitreos Britannos* or 'glassy Britons' (*Amores* 2.16.39). As a final point, it is interesting to note that the original inhabitants of the land the Romans called Britannia (Greek *Pretanníа*) knew it as Albion (*Pliny Naturalis historia* 4.102) and themselves as *Pretani* or *Priteni*, which possibly means 'the painted (or tattooed) ones'. The name survived as *Picti*, Picts. The term, perhaps one of abuse, was used by the Romans from the late third century onwards to describe the inhabitants of northern Britannia beyond what had been the Antonine Wall (e.g. *XII Panegyrici Latini* 8.11.4, Ammianus 20.1.1, 26.4.5, 27.8.5).

Other bodily adornments would have included personal jewellery, particularly armlets and bracelets commonly worn by all Celts. However, it is the neck-ring or torque that is the attribute par excellence of the Celtic warrior. Extant examples are made of a pliant rod of metal, either plain or twisted, or are tubular in construction. In both cases they are thickened at the ends, with ring or loop terminals for rod torques and buffer terminals for tubular torques. They were fashioned in gold, silver, electrum, iron, or copper alloy according to the status of the wearer. The Caledonii, according to Herodian, adorned 'their necks with iron, considering this ornament as a sign of wealth, just as other barbarians do gold' (3.14.7). Obviously some warriors wore iron torques, but the handsome torque-terminal from Shaw Hill, Peebleshire, implies gold was the metal of choice for others.

In their ethnographic observations of the Celts it seems our ancient authors were mistaken in thinking they wore no clothes, although some warriors might well have stripped for battle. The Gaesatae are the exemplars of this tradition, a fanatic warrior group of young unmarried males who stood outside the tribal system and invariably hired themselves out as mercenaries. The Graeco-Roman authors invariably mention three articles of clothing, namely long breeches (*bracae*), long sleeved, thigh-length tunics (*tunicae*) and heavyweight or lightweight woollen cloaks (*saga*). Diodoros, when describing the Gauls, says (5.30.1) their apparel was conspicuous because of the material having been dyed and embroidered in varied hues. This is confirmed by items of clothing recovered from Celtic graves and Iron Age bog-bodies. Clothes were made of wool or linen (flax), brightly coloured and set with checked or tweed-like designs; however, owing to the use of vegetable dyes, much of the colour would have become subdued fairly quickly. A woollen cloth fragment from Falkirk, dated to circa AD 100, is woven into a simple check pattern. Other archaeological finds have also shown the presence of white and coloured sheep's wool in cloth that had not been dyed. One sample of white cloth from Hallstatt in Austria had woven into it a rectangular pattern of bands of black or dark brown wool. The use of black wool is attested by Tacitus' description of the women who stood with the druids against C. Suetonius Paulinus and his army, on the southern shore of Môn (Anglesey) in AD 61, 'dressed in robes of deathly black … in the style of the Furies' (*Annales* 14.30). The finds from peat-bogs also demonstrate that the check pattern did not always depend on contrasting dyed or natural yarns, but sometimes on yarns with contrasted spin-directions instead – the subtle 'shadow checks'.

The Antonine Wall ditch at Watling Lodge, looking west. Here the berm, the open space between the ditch and the rampart, is well preserved. This served as a precaution both against the rampart slipping into the ditch and it being undermined by any excessive erosion of the ditch sides. (Author's collection)

The Gask Ridge

The evidence for the Gask 'frontier' comprises a line of forts, fortlets and watchtowers along a military road. This is an arrangement that physically resembles the *limes* of Trajan (once thought to belong to Domitian) in the Taunus and Wetterau between Lahn and the Main, some 30 miles (*c.* 48km) east of the Rhine. This re-dating thus makes the Gask Ridge, if indeed it is a *limes*, the earliest known example in the empire of an artificial frontier placed under permanent surveillance, which was built 40 years before Hadrian's Wall and 60 years before the Antonine Wall. As currently known, it begins at Glenbank, just to the north of Dunblane and ends at Bertha, just upstream of Perth on the Tay. For much of its length, it runs along the prominent Gask Ridge on the northern side of Strathearn in Perthshire, hence its name.

The Gask Ridge, which rises some 70m above sea level, lies between the Highland massif and the peninsula of Fife, and forms part of a corridor northward towards the coastal strip of richer agricultural land that extends to the Moray Firth. The ridge itself is an east–west spine of land just north of the River Earn with fine views north towards Glenalmond, as well as back into the hollow of Strathearn.

Anatomy

Where it passed along the Gask Ridge the military road was flanked by no fewer than 11 watchtowers (*burgi*) at roughly one Roman mile intervals, placed a little way to one or other side of the road. Presumably there was a cleared strip of land on either side of the road. The free-standing watchtowers were of a standard plan, with sides some 3m (*c.* 10 Roman feet) long with substantial timber uprights at the four corners, which probably supported a structure two storeys high. An earth rampart and one or two penannular ditches, with a gap to allow access from the road, enclosed each watchtower. The upcast from the ditch was used to form a low counter-scarp bank.

The watchtower detachment strength cannot be proved, but a single *contubernium*, or messing-unit, of eight men could have adequately performed all the likely duties of the watch. The tower's ground space of some 100 Roman feet (*c.* 29.6m) square, with at least one room above, would approximate to the barrack-block space allocated to this sub-unit in a fort.

At Kaims Castle, about halfway between Ardoch and the next fort at Strageath, lies a fortlet, almost square in plan, with sides some 30m long, set within a single, almost circular rampart and ditch. A single gateway faces the military road, which was reached by means of a causeway across the ditch. Kaims Castle was linked to the fort at Ardoch by means of three watchtowers. Another watchtower north of the fortlet suggests a link with the fort at Strageath, and that in turn guarded the western end of the group of watchtowers along the Gask Ridge.

One more fortlet lies at Glenbank, to the south of Ardoch near Greenloaning. Positioned just south of the military road, the fortlet is surrounded by a double ditch-system and has a single gateway, with traces of a four-post gatehouse structure, facing north-west towards the road. The site itself sits on a very slight mound with excellent views to the north, east and west and a somewhat poorer view to the south, where it faces gently rising ground. Of a similar size to that at Kaims Castle, the fortlet was large enough to accommodate a single century (*centuria*) of 80 men.

As already noted, the Gask 'frontier system' also includes three forts, those at Ardoch, Strageath and Bertha. Although its visible remains date to the period

The Antonine Wall ditch at Croy Hill, here hewn from the hard basalt of which the hill is largely composed. The ditch appears as an irregular cut on the north flank of Croy Hill, which is so steep hereabouts that formal defence seems hardly necessary. In the distance is Bar Hill. (Author's collection)

when it became an outpost fort for the Antonine frontier system, Agricola established Ardoch, possibly during his third campaign season (AD 79). Six miles (9.6km) north-east of Ardoch lies Strageath, which was also an Agricolan foundation re-commissioned as an outpost fort of the Antonine Wall, overlooking the River Earn. Between this fort and the next, that found at Bertha, runs the Gask Ridge. Bertha lies at the confluence of the River Almond and the Tay, and the Agricolan fort here was the largest of the three, some 9.5 acres (c. 3.8 ha) in area compared to about 8.6 acres (c. 3.5 ha) occupied by the fort at Ardoch. The site was reoccupied in the Antonine period, as attested by an altar (*RIB* 2213c) dedicated to *Disciplina Augusti*, and was the most northerly outpost fort of the Antonine Wall.

Function

Establishing a 'frontier system' north of the Forth–Clyde line may have been an attempt to enclose the salient of good arable land that lies between the Forth and the Tay. Alternatively, the Gask Ridge could be seen as a temporary launching pad for further conquest; the fort at Bertha, for instance, would have served as an ideal jumping-off point for incursions north into Strathmore. For the Romans, at least until the third century, a good offence was invariably based on a strong defence.

Normally watchtowers had a twofold role: to see and be seen, that is, to serve both as vantage points and signal stations. However, the watchtowers along the Gask Ridge were positioned too close together for signalling purposes and this has led to the suggestion that they formed part of a frontier system. Moreover, the watchtowers did not stand alone. Here they were integrated with forts and fortlets to maintain close surveillance over an extended front, which may originally have been drawn from the Forth to the Tay. Thus news of hostile movements across or along the line (which may partly have coincided with a tribal boundary) would have been passed down the chain of posts with requests for immediate action.

Both the Antonine Wall rampart mound and ditch are well preserved at Seabegs Wood, having now been cleared of the undergrowth that once obscured them. The rampart mound is to the right, with the berm just to its left and in front of the ditch. (Author's collection)

Flavian Forth–Tay 'frontier system'

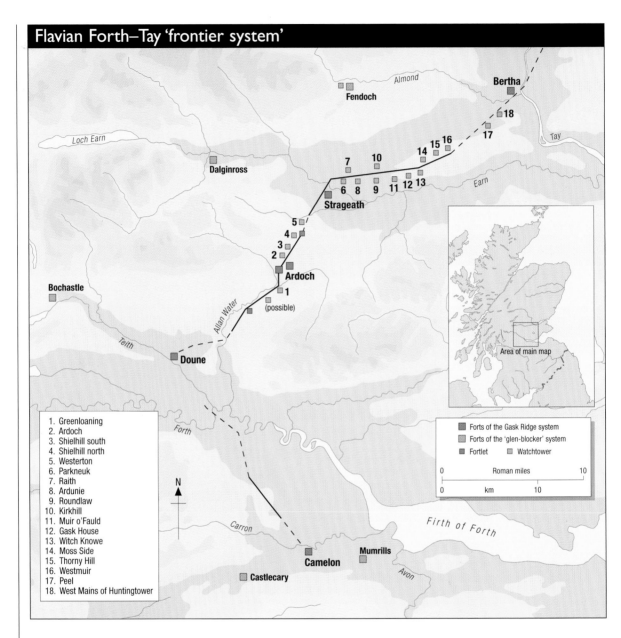

ABOVE The Flavian Forth–Tay 'frontier system', showing the Gask Ridge watchtowers and forts, and 'glen-blocker' forts.

1. Greenloaning
2. Ardoch
3. Shielhill south
4. Shielhill north
5. Westerton
6. Parkneuk
7. Raith
8. Ardunie
9. Roundlaw
10. Kirkhill
11. Muir o'Fauld
12. Gask House
13. Witch Knowe
14. Moss Side
15. Thorny Hill
16. Westmuir
17. Peel
18. West Mains of Huntingtower

Forts of the Gask Ridge system
Forts of the 'glen-blocker' system
Fortlet   Watchtower

0   Roman miles   10
0   km   10

A watchtower of the Gask 'frontier system'

Watchtowers (*burgi*) were generally built of timber and turf, since this was the quickest and most efficient method. Consequently the archaeological evidence is limited usually to post-holes and ramparts. However, a number of square earth-and-timber watchtowers appear on the columns of Trajan (Scene I$_{4, 5, 6}$) and Marcus Aurelius (Scene Id, s), and these provide the basis for the reconstruction shown here. Manned by a single *contubernium* of eight men, the two-storey timber installation is set within a low turf rampart, topped with a wattlework parapet, surrounded by a single penannular ditch and an outer bank of upcast material. There is a single entranceway facing the military road that runs along the spine of the Gask Ridge. Soldiers on duty here are out-posted from the nearby fort at Strageath.

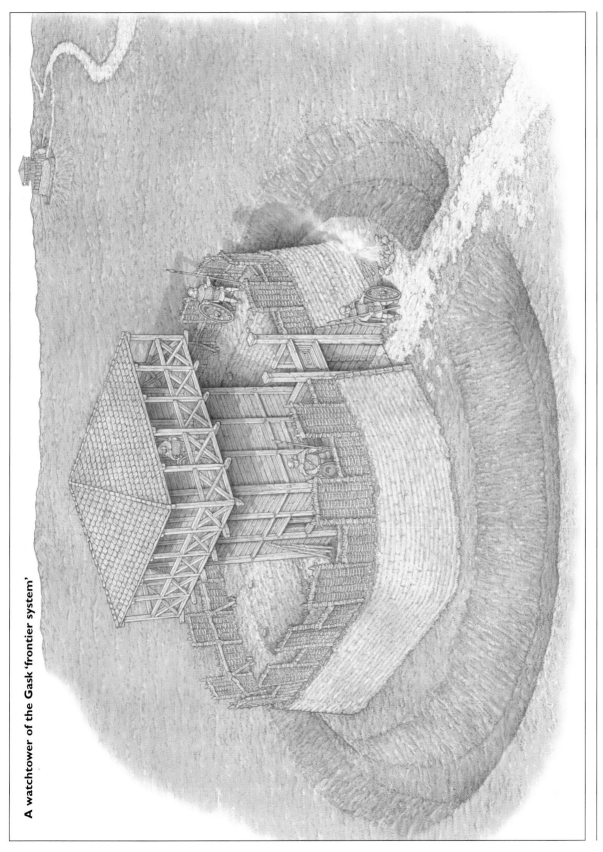

A watchtower of the Gask 'frontier system'

Likewise, movement of people into and out of the province could be regulated. Literary evidence in regard to the Rhine frontier tells us that such movement was governed by regulations (Tacitus *Germania* 41). Travellers could only enter the empire unarmed, under guard, by day, at fixed points and times, and upon payment. Customs-dues were also payable at the frontier, as were charges on trade (Tacitus *Historiae* 4.64–65). The army also helped collect taxes in the frontier zone. Tacitus (*Agricola* 31.1) places in Calgacus' mouth a number of grievances, including direct tax (*tributum*) and the requisition of grain. Normally, within the empire, taxes were paid in cash, but there were people on the margins of the empire who paid in kind. Thus, according to Tacitus (*Annales* 4.72), the Frisii on the north side of the lower Rhine had their taxation assessed in ox hides, which were not only collected by the army but were also earmarked for military purposes.

Case study 3: anatomy of a Flavian fort

Fendoch fort was some 4.5 acres (*c.* 1.8 ha) in area. It was constructed either during the governorship of Agricola or immediately after his recall. It lies at the head of Glenalmond opposite the mouth of the Sma' Glen near Crieff, and so may be one of the 'glen-blockers' whose principle role was to guard against direct attacks from the Highland massif. The site was excavated extensively by Sir Ian Richmond (1936–38), and its layout recovered in such detail that it has often been regarded as a model for the earth-and-timber forts of the Flavian period. The earth ramparts, fronted by a single ditch except on the more vulnerable east side, defined a neat rectangular playing-card shape with rounded corners.

Yet it has differences from other contemporary forts. Fendoch's plan was conventional enough: the central range (*latera praetorii*) consisted of the headquarters building (*principia*), the garrison commander's house (*praetorium*), two granaries (*horrea*), a workshop (*fabrica*) and storage buildings (cf. Richmond who suggested the *fabrica* was in fact a hospital or *valetudinarium*). The forward range (*praetentura*) to the south consisted of four L-shaped barrack-blocks (*centuriae*) and two storage buildings, and the rearward range (*retentura*) to the north consisted of six L-shaped *centuriae*. The 10 *centuriae* each had 10 pairs of

The *principia*, Bar Hill fort, looking diagonally across the covered cross-hall (*basilica*) towards the south. Here the commander of the garrison could address his assembled troops. To the left is the rear range of three rooms, the central one being the *sacellum*, which housed the unit standards, imperial statues and cultic altars. (Author's collection)

rooms for sleeping and equipment (*contubernia*), which suggests, if all this space was utilised, that Fendoch was built for a *cohors milliaria peditata*. A number of stone-built ovens have also been identified. Five in number, set in the back of the ramparts and each at the end of a barrack-block, suggests that each oven served one *centuria*. The fort was exceptionally long – nearly double the width – owing to the nature of the site, which was largely bog-land. It was dismantled with some care only a few years after its construction and was deserted by *c*. AD 90.

Case study 4: anatomy of a Flavian fortlet

During his fourth campaigning season (AD 80) Agricola established a number of military installations along the Forth–Clyde isthmus. Castle Greg, 3.7 miles (6km) south-east of the village of West Calder, was a fortlet (0.3 ha) probably built to monitor an east–west road that may have run along the northern flank of the Pentland Hills and joined the major Clydesdale–Annandale trunk-route at the Bankhead fortlet near Carnwath.

On the ground nowadays is visible a double ditch-system, protecting a rectangular earth rampart. The latter still stands to a height of a metre above the level of the interior and about 1.8m above the bottom of the innermost of the two enclosing ditches. A single entrance pierces the rampart on its east side, where the curving in of the outer ditch to meet the causeway is typical of Flavian earthworks. What are called 'parrot's beak' ditch-terminals created a funnelled approach to the gateway. The area within the fortlet, measuring some 38m by 50m, is remarkably flat. When originally dug, the V-shaped ditches of the fortlet would have been some 3m deep. A split-timber or wattlework parapet, at least 1.5m high, crowned the rampart, with a walkway round it and a timber tower over the gateway. Within there would have been a pair of half-sized barrack-blocks (*centuriae*), housing up to a century (*centuria*) of 80 men. The interior was excavated in 1852 and pottery dating to the Flavian period was recovered from a well in the centre of the fortlet. There are commanding views of the Pentland Hills to the north, and before afforestation of the surrounding area, the position occupied by the fortlet was one of bleak, open moorland.

The fort at Ardoch

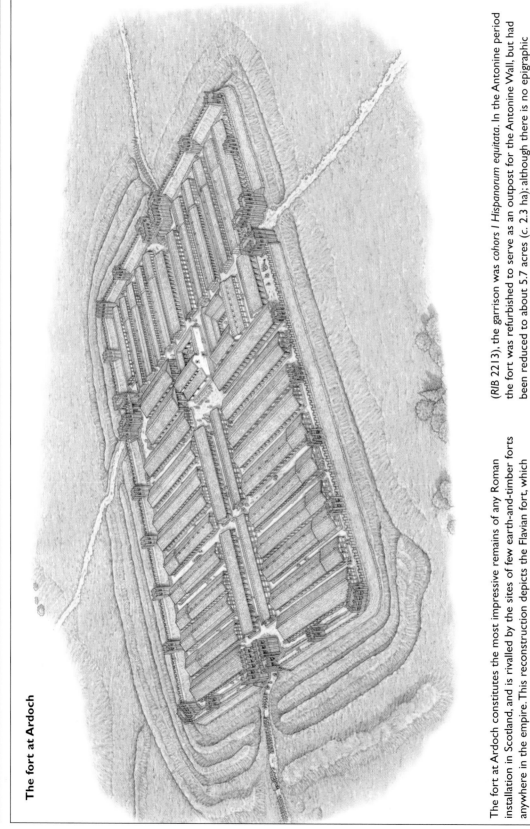

The fort at Ardoch constitutes the most impressive remains of any Roman installation in Scotland, and is rivalled by the sites of few earth-and-timber forts anywhere in the empire. This reconstruction depicts the Flavian fort, which occupied an area of some 8.6 acres (c. 3.5 ha). After the abandonment of Inchtuthil it formed part of the Gask 'frontier system' until that was abandoned in the late 80s. At some stage during this period, according to an extant tombstone (*RIB* 2213), the garrison was *cohors I Hispanorum equitata*. In the Antonine period the fort was refurbished to serve as an outpost for the Antonine Wall, but had been reduced to about 5.7 acres (c. 2.3 ha); although there is no epigraphic evidence of the second century garrison, there was sufficient room for a *cohors milliaria equitata*. It is possible that the *Alauna Veniconum* entry from Claudius Ptolemaeus (*Geographia* 2.3.9) may be identified with the Ardoch site.

The *lilia* just north of the Antonine Wall at Rough Castle, so-called by the soldiers because of a resemblance to the lily with its vertical stem and enclosing leaves. Arranged in checkerboard configuration, these pitfalls (of 10 rows, with over 20 in each) once contained sharpened stakes (*cippi*) camouflaged with twigs and foliage. (Esther Carré)

The Antonine Wall ditch west of Rough Castle. On the left of the ditch is a low mound, all that remains of the turf rampart that once stood at a height of 2.75m. This was topped with a 1.85m-wide wooden duckboard walkway protected by a split-timber or wattlework parapet 1.5m high. (Author's collection)

The Antonine conquest and consolidation

The ideology of *imperium sine fine*, an empire without limit, was central to the Roman stereotype of a good emperor. Suetonius' analysis of Claudius' motives for the invasion of Britannia boiled down to the simple fact that it 'was the place where a legitimate triumph could be most readily earned' (*Divus Claudius* 17.1). Antoninus Pius, the most unwarlike of emperors, also appreciated the force of the ideology and gave great publicity to the fairly ordinary military achievement of his reign when the frontier in Britannia was advanced. Indeed, Graeco-Roman authors of the period still spoke in the Roman tradition. Aelius Aristides, a Greek orator living during the reign of Antoninus Pius, praises Rome because 'you recognised no fixed boundaries, nor does another dictate to what point your control reaches' (*Ad Roma* 10).

The very idea of the frontier as a line on a map is modern. It was Napoleon, for instance, who said 'the frontiers of nations are either large rivers, chains of mountains, or deserts' (*Military Maxims* 1). Roman frontiers (*limites*), on the other hand, were never linear but were always zones. Fuzzy and interlocking, these zones might be defined by four groups of people: Roman military, Roman non-military, indigenous peoples (or 'friendlies'), and non-indigenous peoples (or 'barbarians'). Thus a frontier (*limes*) was a wide strip of terrain within which Roman troops exercised not just military control but also social and economic functions crucial to the safety and efficiency of the *limes* and adjacent territories. The borders of other people were never inviolable boundaries, and the emperor was always ready to cross them if it was in his interest to do so. Hence the slogan 'A king has been given to the Quadi' is one of the few publicised acts of foreign policy on the coins of Antoninus Pius (*RIC* Antoninus Pius 620). Despite the ideological recognition that the Danube was some sort of geopolitical dividing line from the time of Augustus (*Res Gestae Divi Augusti* 30.2, Strabo 6.4.2), Antoninus Pius carefully cultivated and controlled relations with the 'barbarians' beyond the Danube.

Imperial policy in northern Britannia

Precisely when the Romans first ventured north of the Tyne–Solway line is a matter of debate. Since the reign of Claudius, the security of northern Britannia had been founded on a treaty between Rome and the Brigantian queen, Cartimandua. In AD 69, however, her consort Venutius ousted Cartimandua and friendly relations between Rome and the Brigantes came to an abrupt end. In the cutting words of Tacitus, 'the kingdom was left to Venutius, the war to us' (*Historiae* 3.45). At a time of civil war in the empire, the governor, M. Vettius Bolanus, was able to do little more than rescue the pro-Roman queen. There are hints of rather more military activity during his period of office (AD 69–71) than Tacitus allows (*Agricola* 8.1, 16.5), but it seems highly improbable that Vettius Bolanus operated in 'the Caledonian plains' as Statius, in a poem written to Vettius Bolanus' son Vettius Crispinus, implies (*Silvae* 5.2.140-49). In the early 90s, when the poem was first published, Caledonia was news. If the adjective 'Brigantian' is read instead, the scene of Vettius Bolanus' operations is more credibly defined. The territory occupied by this confederacy of northern tribes is known from places mentioned by Claudius Ptolemaeus (*Geographia* 2.3.16) and from the locations of Roman inscriptions to Brigantia, the goddess of the Brigantes (e.g. *ILS* 4718, *RIB* 2091). As such it extended from a little north of the Tyne–Solway isthmus to, excluding Humberside, the rivers Mersey and Trent in the south.

In the bathhouse, the bather entered first a cold room, and then proceeded through rooms of increasingly higher temperatures. Thereafter he retraced his steps to the cold room, where water splashed over the body served to close up the pores before he dressed and exited the bathhouse. Often there was a hot-dry room (*laconicum*), as here at Bar Hill fort – note the *hypocaust*. (Author's collection)

The arrival in AD 71 of the new governor, Q. Petillius Cerialis, together with *legio II Adiutrix pia fidelis*, saw renewed activity in the territory of the Brigantes. Tacitus (*Agricola* 17.1) refers to Petillius Cerialis winning not altogether bloodless battles against the Brigantes after campaigning widely in their territory. Although Tacitus passes over this campaign rather briefly, the foundation of Eboracum (York) as a legionary fortress is usually attributed to Petillius Cerialis. There is no epigraphic or literary confirmation of this, but the most graphic evidence for the scale of his activities in the territory of the Brigantes comes from Luguvalium (Carlisle) where the oak timbers of the primary fort were felled, according to dendrochronology, during the winter of AD 72/73. This date was corroborated by finds of early Flavian pottery and coins from elsewhere in Carlisle as well as the fort itself. Luguvalium, suffice to say, would have served as a convenient bridgehead for an advance into Scotland.

Whilst Tacitus has a tendency to underplay the achievements of earlier governors, credit for the attempted subjugation of northern Britannia is rightly attributed to Cn. Iulius Agricola, Tacitus' father-in-law and governor of Britannia for seven 'action-packed' years (AD 77–84). By building upon the successes of his energetic military predecessors, especially those of Petillius Cerialis (whom he had served under for three years as legate of *legio XX Valeria Victrix*), Agricola's campaigns in northern Britannia appear to reflect an imperial policy aimed towards the conquest of the whole island. This view is consistent with the pattern of activity of all of the governors, each in his own way a hard-headed and ambitious soldier, who served in the province under the Flavian emperors (Vespasian, AD 69–79; Titus, AD 79–81; Domitian, AD 81–96).

On the other hand, it can be argued that Agricola had no intention of entering the Highland massif, as the valleys leading from this were carefully blocked by forts at Drumquhassle (above Loch Lomond), Malling (south shore of the Lake of Menteith), Bochastle (below the pass of Leny), Dalginross (head of Strathearn) and Fendoch (mouth of the Sma' Glen), while a legionary fortress was established at Inchtuthil (below the Tay gorge at Dunkeld). This would suggest that the policy was to prevent the Caledonii from breaking into lowland Scotland by creating a *cordon militaire*. Whatever the grand plan, however, it was never allowed to be brought to fruition. Agricola was recalled (AD 84) and Domitian soon ordered withdrawal (AD 86). The abandonment of the newly won territory by the emperor was castigated by Tacitus, who bitterly comments that 'Britannia was conquered and immediately abandoned'

The fortress at Inchtuthil

The legionary base at Inchtuthil, on the Tay 15km (9.5 miles) north of Perth (where the river is tidal), was never rebuilt in masonry, and was abandoned in AD 86 before the initial timber-phase was completed. Although the bulk of the construction was achieved under his successor, the decision to plant a fortress here was Agricola's. The fortress was to be occupied for less than three years by *legio XX Valeria Victrix*, the unit Agricola had commanded earlier in his career. Covering an area of 53.5 acres (21.7

ha), the fortress sits on an isolated plateau, about 45m above sea level, within a widening of the Tay's alluvial plain. As this reconstruction shows, a turf rampart (**1**, with later stone facing), ditch (**2**) and counter-scarp bank (**3**) defend it. There are four timber gateways (A, B, C and D). Within the defences are 64 barrack-blocks (**4**, *centuriae*) that house the legion's 54 centuries (*centuriae*) of nine *cohortes quingenariae* (*cohortes II–IX*) and five 'double-strength' *centuriae* of the *cohors milliaria* (*cohors prima*, **4a**). Alongside

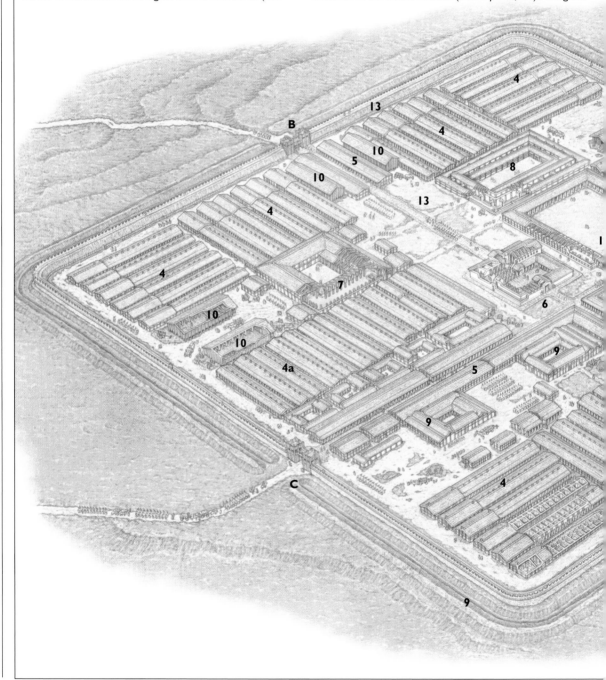

these are over 170 store-buildings (**5**), a small headquarters building (**6**, *principia*), a large workshop (**7**, *fabrica*), hospital (**8**, *valetudinarium*), four tribunes' houses (**9**), six granaries (**10**, *horrea*), and a drill-hall (**11**, *basilica exercitatoria*). All the accommodation for the legionaries and their daily affairs has thus been erected. There is a prepared site for the legate's residence (**12**, *praetorium*) and bathhouse (**13**, *balneum*), and room for three or four more tribunes' houses and two more *horrea*. A larger *principia* would

probably have been built, presumably in masonry, following the completion of the timber-framed buildings. Before it was finished the fortress was systematically demolished, but the stone extramural bathhouse and the stone facing of the rampart suggest there was an initial intention of permanence, probably serving as the command base for the 'glen-blocker' forts. It is possible that the *Pinnata Castra* entry from Claudius Ptolemaeus (*Geographia* 2.3.13) may be identified as Inchtuthil.

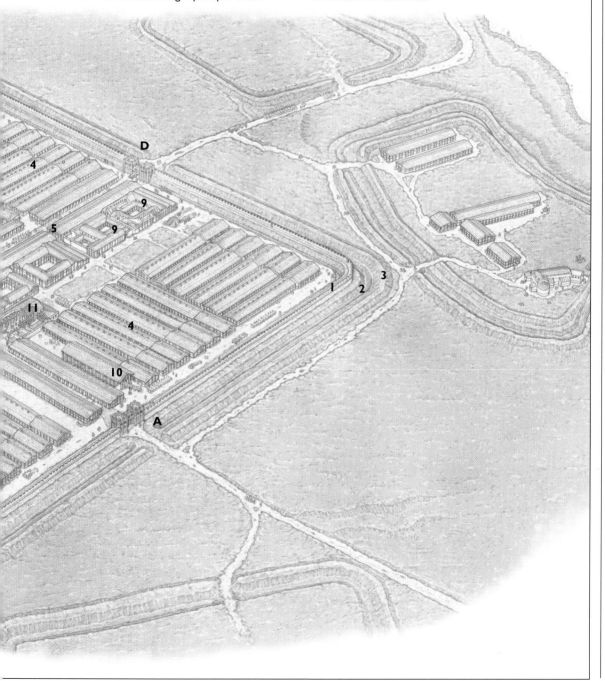

The multiplication of defensive ditches (five in all) on the north and east sides of Ardoch fort is the result of successive reductions in its size and not of anxiety over its security. Initially the fort had an area of some 3.5 ha, but by the close of the Antonine period it had been reduced to about 2.3 ha. (Author's collection)

The five, still crisp, defensive ditches on the east side of Ardoch fort, with the causeway from the east gateway (*porta principalis dextra*) that crosses them. The rampart mound of the smaller Antonine fort is clearly visible on the right, while the outer three ditches belong to that of the Flavian period. (Author's collection)

(*Historiae* 1.2, cf. *Agricola* 10.1). His meaning is that Mons Graupius clinched the conquest and the jealousy of Domitian threw it away.

In truth the emperor and his advisors were well aware that the far north was going to tie down too many soldiers for too long in a futile attempt to confront an intractable foe that spent its time disappearing into marshes and forests. In fact Tacitus, in a throwaway line, passed over the secret of the northern tribes when he said, 'had not the marshes and the forests covered the fugitives that victory would have ended the war' (*Agricola* 26.2). Winston Churchill once dubbed the sites of battles as the 'punctuation marks of history', but history does not judge Mons Graupius 'a Hastings' and questions whether Agricola's depleted force could have won one. Legionary *vexillationes* are known to have been taken from all four legions (*ILS* 1025, 9200, cf. Tacitus *Agricola* 26.1) to supply Domitian with reinforcements for his war against the Chatti in Germania Superior (AD 82). Moreover, other events elsewhere in the empire, namely a major Dacian incursion across the Danube, prevented the total occupation of Britannia. Consequently *legio II Adiutrix pia fidelis* would be withdrawn for service on the Danube (*ILS* 9193, cf. 2719), leaving the garrison of Britannia permanently reduced from four to three legions (AD 86). Despite the Tacitean condemnation, the realities of the situation were understood in Rome. The new conquests could not be held through lack of manpower and so the retreat to the Forth–Clyde line was probably rapid, but the area to the south of this was relinquished more slowly.

Following the abandonment of gains beyond the Forth–Clyde isthmus, according to the archaeological record much of lowland Scotland remained in occupation. However, further forts had been given up by AD 105 and the Stanegate (literally 'stony street', cf. Old Norse *stane* 'stone', and *gata* 'road'), the Agricolan military road built to cover much of the distance between the Tyne and the Solway, became an important element of the frontier zone. A slightly irregular system of forts was spaced along its length from Coria (Corbridge) to Luguvalium (Carlisle), and at some stage fortlets were introduced in at least two places (Haltwhistle Burn, Throp) between the forts. Although it cannot be regarded as a true frontier system, the Stanegate marks the northern limit of military occupation in Britannia until Hadrian recognised the need for an artificial barrier and ordered the construction of what was to become the most elaborate and best known of all Roman frontier systems.

Origins of the Antonine Wall

A reference in Pausanias (8.43.4) to trouble amongst the Brigantes during the reign of Antoninus Pius may provide the clue to the nature of the trouble that stimulated the campaign in northern Britannia:

> Also he [Antoninus Pius] deprived the Brigantes in Britannia of most of their territory because they had taken up arms and invaded the Genounian district (?), of which the people are subject to the Romans.

Until recently this was identified as the occasion for the abandonment of the Antonine conquests in the late 150s. However, Pausanias' comment appears as part of a description of all the wars fought in the emperor's reign; it seems hardly credible that the re-conquest of lowland Scotland should have been overlooked in favour of a minor tribal revolt. The decision to abandon Hadrian's Wall and to advance the frontier of the province more than 70 miles coincided with the accession of Antoninus Pius, as well as the arrival of a new governor, the energetic Q. Lollius Urbicus, previously governor of Germania Inferior. An inscribed stone (*RIB* 1147) from Corbridge proves that Lollius Urbicus was in Britannia as governor as early as AD 139, the year after Antoninus Pius became emperor (10 July AD 138).

Despite Pausanias' contemporary evidence the reasons for this dramatic change of imperial policy are not obvious, but the suggested parallel with the position of Claudius on his accession is, however, convincing. Antoninus Pius, who had no direct personal military experience and was Hadrian's second choice as the successor (25 February AD 138), needed to establish his credibility with the army and thus gain military prestige. Claudius, too, lacked military experience and went so far as personally participating in the closing stages of the invasion of Britannia (AD 43) with the sole

This farm track from Muir o' Fauld follows the line of the military road that once crossed the Gask Ridge. Placed a little way to one side or another, watchtowers flanked the road at roughly one-Roman-mile intervals and commanded fine views, now obscured by forestry, both to the north and south. (Author's collection)

purpose of acquiring military laurels to bolster his political position with the populace and the army. Indeed, it was the only occasion of his reign, despite frontier advances into Germania and probably North Africa, that Antoninus Pius accepted the imperial acclamation for a victory as imperator (*CIL* 10.515), which was then celebrated on a series of coin issues (*RIC* Antoninus Pius 743–45). The point had been made, and the dignified emperor who never left Italy or saw an army would be subsequently remembered, in a panegyric on Constantius Chlorus (delivered in AD 297), 'for having brought the war in Britannia to completion' (*XII Panegyrici Latini* 8.14).

As these coins are dated to the end of AD 142, it seems logical to assume that the reoccupation of lowland Scotland occurred then. The new frontier system across the Forth–Clyde isthmus is dated by two inscriptions (*RIB* 2191–92) found at Balmuildy: each bear the name of Lollius Urbicus and it is assumed that commencement under this governor started no later than AD 143, the year he left the province. Of the Roman forts in Scotland that have been

Table 2: Auxiliary inscriptions from Antonine Wall forts (after Hanson and Maxwell 1986: table 8.3)

Fort	Building inscription[1]	Altar	Tombstone
Mumrills		*ala I Tungrorum* (RIB 2140)	Nectovelius, a soldier of *cohors II Thracum eq* (RIB 2142)
Rough Castle	*cohors VI Nerviorum* (RIB 2145)	*cohors VI Nerviorum* (RIB 2144)[2]	
Castlecary	*cohors I Tungrorum milliaria* (RIB 2155)	*cohors I fida Vardullorum milliaria eq cR* (RIB 2149)	
Bar Hill	*cohors I Baetasiorum cR* (RIB 2170)	1. *cohors I Hamiorum sagittaria* (RIB 2167) 2. *cohors I Baetasiorum cR* (RIB 2169)	C. Iulius Marcellinus, prefect of *cohors I Hamiorum sagittaria* (RIB 2172)
Balmuildy		Caecilius Nepos, a tribune of an unspecified unit (RIB 2189)	
Castlehill		*cohors IIII Gallorum eq* (RIB 2195)	
Old Kilpatrick		*cohors I Baetasiorum cR* (RIB 2213B)	

Notes:

[1] Building records from the reoccupation phase of the Wall (Antonine II, c. AD 158–164).

[2] Commanded by Flavius Betto, a centurion of *legio XX Valeria Victrix*.

The bathhouse in the fort-annexe at Bearsden, Antonine Wall, looking north-east. This is the apsidal cold-plunge bath immediately off the bathhouse's cold room (*fridarium*). After undressing, and before proceeding to the hot rooms, bathers would enter this unheated room and plunge into the cold water. (Esther Carré)

The bathhouse, in the north-west corner of Bar Hill fort, on the Antonine Wall. One of the capstones from the furnace's main flue has been placed to indicate its original position. This furnace (*praefurnium*) provided heat to the three nearest rooms. In the centre – note the *hypocaust* – was the hot-dry room (*laconicum*) heated by an independent furnace. (Esther Carré)

examined, including those on the Antonine Wall, most have provided evidence of two distinct periods of occupation (Antonine I and II). These are attested either epigraphically, where two different auxiliary units are recorded for the same site (e.g. Mumrills, Castlecary, Bar Hill), or structurally, where buildings within a fort can be shown to have been rebuilt (e.g. Rough Castle, Castlecary, Bar Hill).

The end of the first occupation came at some time late in the 150s, possibly in AD 158. An inscription (*RIB* 1322) from Newcastle-upon-Tyne records the arrival of reinforcements for all three legions of Britannia from the garrisons of Germania Superior and Germania Inferior under a new governor, Cn. Iulius Verus. The exact date of his arrival is uncertain, but he was certainly in office in AD 158. It is quite likely that Iulius Verus came directly from the governorship of Germania Inferior, possibly bringing these *vexillationes* with him to assist in what appears to be yet another revolt in northern Britannia. It is conjectured that Iulius Verus supervised a withdrawal from lowland Scotland after the uprising had been finally quelled.

Whatever the truth of the matter, the interval between abandonment and reoccupation of the Antonine Wall was only brief. Inscriptions from Rough Castle, Castlecary and Bar Hill (*RIB* 2145, 2155, 2170) all record building by auxiliaries, and thus ought to relate to the second period of occupation, yet all are dedicated to Antoninus Pius. This second occupation ended in AD 164, pulling the frontier back southward to Hadrian's Wall, which was to remain so until the Roman withdrawal from Britannia in the early fifth century. Thus the Antonine Wall marked the northern frontier of the empire for little more than 20 years.

The Antonine Wall

Built from east to west, the whole of the new frontier system ran from Bridgeness on the south bank of the Forth to Old Kilpatrick on the north bank of the Clyde, a distance of a little over 37 miles (40.5 Roman miles) across the Forth–Clyde isthmus. Carefully positioned on the southern side of the Kelvin and Carron valleys, the Antonine Wall had a fine outlook northward towards the Campsie Fells and the Kilsyth Hills, and further east, across the marshlands of the Forth.

Anatomy

In the *Scriptores Historiae Augustae* (Antoninus Pius 5.4) the Antonine Wall is clearly referred to as a *murus caespiticius*, that is, a turf wall:

> [Antoninus Pius] through his legate Lollius Urbicus, also conquered the Britons, driving off barbarians and building another wall, this time of turf.

This terse but explicit comment leaves us in no doubt that it was a matter of note that the new frontier system had not been made of stone.

The archaeological evidence shows that the rampart of the Antonine Wall was built mainly of cut turf blocks standing on a stone base, 4.25–4.9m wide, formed of two outer rows of squared kerbstones with a mass of rough unshaped stones packed in between. At intervals the stone base had culverts incorporated in it. In this it differed from the turf-built sector of Hadrian's Wall (Turf Wall), which was based directly upon the ground. The innovation, undoubtedly adopted as a result of experience gained, would have afforded a more stable base for the turf superstructure and would have greatly improved drainage. Likewise it was only two-thirds the width of its predecessor, the Turf Wall, thus saving materials and time.

With its sloping back and front, the turf superstructure was probably no more than 2.75m high with a 1.85m-wide wooden duckboard walkway protected by a split-timber or wattlework parapet some 1.5m high. The latter type of

On the high ground west of the trunk road (A822) into the Sma' Glen and north-west of Fendoch fort lies a watchtower. Enjoying a good forward view northward up the Glen, the timber watchtower was set with an earth rampart and a single ditch, which was broken by an entrance on the south-east side facing the fort. (Author's collection)

breastwork seems inherently more likely as the woven wattlework hurdles, of hazel or willow, would have been easy and quick to make. Access to the walkway may have been by way of wooden ladders, either movable or fixed. It should certainly not be assumed, on the basis of a comparison with Hadrian's Wall, that a turf rampart was necessarily intended as a temporary measure. It was the construction of Hadrian's Wall in stone that was the exception.

To the north of the rampart there was a ditch. The open space between the two, called the berm, was seldom less than 6.1m wide. The ditch was, like most Roman military ditches, V-shaped in profile, the scarp and counter-scarp sloping up at an angle of circa 30 degrees to the vertical. In places along its length there are indications of a square cleaning-channel (or 'ankle-breaker') at the bottom. The dimensions of the ditch vary from point to point, but the average is about 12.2m and 3.66m deep. The upcast from the ditch was thrown out on its north side where it formed a substantial barrier in its own right. Where the ditch occupied a northwards slope, the upcast served to heighten the north face of the ditch and thus brought the faces to the same level.

The third linear element in the frontier system was the so-called Military Way, the metalled service road that ran roughly parallel to the rampart some 46m to the south. Surviving sections indicate that it was of standard construction, some 4.9–5.5m wide with a pronounced camber and drainage ditches on either side. Additionally, aerial photography not only highlights its course, but also reveals the flanking oblong pits from which the stone and gravel were quarried to build it.

Unlike Hadrian's Wall to the south, the Antonine Wall had a series of regularly spaced forts right from the very beginning. These would house detachments (vexillationes) of legionaries and auxiliary troops. The original plan of the Wall called for six forts, now referred to as the primary forts, widely spaced 6–8 miles (9.6–12.8km) apart, that is, set half a day's march apart. Yet after the Wall had been constructed as far as Castlehill, only 4 miles (6.4km) from its western terminal point, the plan was revised to more than triple the number of forts to the 19 we know of, or suspect, today.

To date, the sites of 17 forts are securely known along the line of the Wall, and two more, namely Inveravon and Falkirk, are suspected on grounds of spacing. The spacing between the forts suggests that it was the intention to dispose them at approximately 1.5 to 3 mile (2.4–4.8km) intervals, which represents a closer spacing of garrisons than on any other frontier of the empire. This new arrangement, therefore, provided a much tighter surveillance

The kingpin of the whole Flavian system in Scotland, the legionary fortress at Inchtuthil, occupied an area of 21.7 ha. Today there is nothing to be seen in the interior of the site, as the internal structures were timber-built. However, this shot, taken from the southern defences, gives an impression of the area covered by the fortress. (Author's collection)

The Antonine Wall

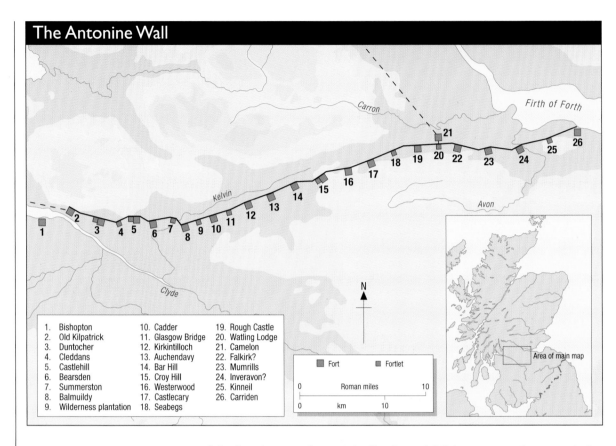

1. Bishopton	10. Cadder	19. Rough Castle
2. Old Kilpatrick	11. Glasgow Bridge	20. Watling Lodge
3. Duntocher	12. Kirkintilloch	21. Camelon
4. Cleddans	13. Auchendavy	22. Falkirk?
5. Castlehill	14. Bar Hill	23. Mumrills
6. Bearsden	15. Croy Hill	24. Inveravon?
7. Summerston	16. Westerwood	25. Kinneil
8. Balmuildy	17. Castlecary	26. Carriden
9. Wilderness plantation	18. Seabegs	

The Antonine Wall, as constructed. Note that only certain fortlets are shown: others presumably existed at one-mile intervals.

of the frontier zone than originally planned. With one exception, namely Bar Hill, all the forts abutted the inner face of the Wall-rampart.

The vast majority of the forts have turf ramparts on a stone base resembling the Wall-rampart, although varying in basal width from 3.7–6.1m. Balmuildy and Castlecary are the two exceptions with a stone curtain-wall, basal width 2.3m and 2.4m respectively. A wooden duckboard walkway and split-timber or wattlework parapet, about 1.5m high, presumably surmounted the turf ramparts to facilitate defence should it ever have been necessary, or in the case of the two stone-walled forts stone parapet and merlons. That such provision was made in fort defences is shown by its depiction on Trajan's Column (scenes XX, XXXII, CX), while at Bearsden burnt wattles, mainly of willow, were found in front of the fort's east rampart.

All forts (except Balmuildy and Castlecary) had four timber-built gateways, each of which was fortified with two flanking-towers. Their lookout platforms were probably not roofed and were accessed by fixed ladder. At the corners of the forts too there were timber towers (*turres*), which did not project in front of their ramparts but were flushed with them and extended to the rear. Again, such defensive features are admirably illustrated on Trajan's Column (scenes XVIII, LI).

All the excavated forts (except Bearsden) had principal buildings in the central range (*latera praetorii*), and most had barrack-blocks (*centuriae*) in the forward (*praetentura*) and rearward (*retentura*) ranges. The principal buildings were usually of local stone, with red-tiled roofs (*tegulae, imbrices*). These included the headquarters building (*principia*), containing an open courtyard, a covered cross-hall (*basilica*) and a range of small rooms at the back to accommodate pay and record clerks, the central room of which was the 'shrine of the standards' (*sacellum*). There was also the garrison commander's house (*praetorium*) as well as the granaries (*horrea*), the latter distinguished by their buttressed walls strong enough to support massive roofs. Other buildings, particularly the *centuriae*, were

LEFT This sculptural relief of three legionaries was found at Croy Hill on the Antonine Wall. It was probably the upper-part of a tombstone showing a father (the deceased) flanked by his two sons. All three presumably served in *legio VI Victrix*, the unit responsible for constructing this part of the Wall. (Esther Carré)

BELOW The Roman road, Dere Street – identified by the darker vegetation as it ascends Soutra Hill towards the wind-farm – looking south from the monastic ruin of Soutra Aisle. Dere Street is attributed in its earliest form to Agricola's campaigns and it remained a major route from York to the Firth of Forth throughout the Roman period and beyond. (Esther Carré)

timber-framed, with wattle-and-daub walling, wooden roofs (oak roofing-shingles) and beaten earth floors. Willow or hazel was a good timber for the wattles, and after the clay had been applied and plastered the building was almost indistinguishable from a stone construction.

The anatomy of the Wall also included a number of smaller fortifications or fortlets, measuring about 18–21m internally and defended by ditches on their east, south and west sides. Smaller than most first-century examples, these fortlets would have been manned by garrisons not more than half a century strong. Although the sequence is not yet fully understood – nine are known to date – it seems likely that these fortlets occurred at regular intervals, possibly about one Roman mile as was the case along Hadrian's Wall, which suggests there were about 40 fortlets in total.

No towers (cf. turrets on Hadrian's Wall) have yet been discovered on the Antonine Wall, but other small structures are known. There are six 'expansions', which survive in pairs and may have served as signalling platforms. They consisted of a turf platform, some 5.2–5.5m square, resting on a stone base and set against the inner face of the rampart of the Wall. At one (Bonnyside East), traces of burning lay beside the platform, together with some shards of Roman pottery. It has been suggested that fires had been lit on top of the expansion, and that the expansions worked in pairs to send signals north and south of the Wall. This

The impressive length of the southern defences at Inchtuthil, comprising ditch, berm, and rampart mound (left to right). The rampart was initially of clay and turf, but later received a stone revetment, left unfinished on the abandonment of the site. (Author's collection)

The surviving earthworks at Inchtuthil are not striking, but this conspicuous hollow marks the broad east ditch of the legionary fortress, looking north-east. Although now flat-bottomed, the ditch was originally V-shaped in profile, 2m deep and 6.1m wide. (Author's collection)

theory is plausible on topographical grounds, for the four eastern expansions (Tentfield East, Tentfield West, Bonnyside East, Bonnyside West) do look northwards over open country while the western two (Croy Hill East, Croy Hill West) look south up Clydesdale. Such installations are well illustrated on the columns of Trajan (Scene I_4) and Marcus Aurelius (Scene Ic). It is also possible, though, that the burning was caused by fires lit by soldiers in hearths in the ground while they were at the site undertaking some other kind of activity.

Also associated with the Wall were a number of forts, both outposts to the north and a network of forts in the hinterland to the south. The latter, such as the fort at Newstead, occupied positions along the main communications routes in southern Scotland, often on sites used by Agricola's troops. Those to the north of the Wall, the old Agricolan forts of Ardoch, Strageath and Bertha, were probably intended to close off, or protect, the peninsula of Fife, whose inhabitants (from the archaeological record a culturally distinct grouping) seem to have been afforded some protection by Rome. The soldiers of these refurbished installations could also monitor the local situation and feed back intelligence to the garrison on the Wall.

To complete this survey of the Antonine Wall a brief note should be made of the numerous temporary camps that lay within its immediate vicinity, which presumably housed the labour force responsible for the construction of the frontier system. These labour camps consisted of large rectangular enclosures surrounded by a rampart and ditch, within which rows of leather tents (*papiliones*) were erected.

Construction

The whole frontier system was built by detachments of all three legions in Britannia, that is, *vexillationes* from the *legiones II Augusta, VI Victrix pia fidelis* and *XX Valeria Victrix*. As many as 20 of their distance slabs survive, elaborately embellished inscriptions that record the lengths of the Wall-rampart completed by the legionary work-parties engaged in building the Antonine frontier system. As far as is known, they were set up at either end of each stint, possibly one stone in each face of the rampart, so that at each junction between the two parties there could originally have been as many as four stones, two facing north and two facing south. The presence of small dovetail clamp-holes in several of the slabs indicates they were originally set in some form of masonry surround. Each slab bore, after the imperial dedication, the identity of the legion and the exact length of the rampart completed.

Within the individual legionary sectors the work would have been divided into smaller lengths allocated to cohorts and centuries under their respective centurions. On Hadrian's Wall it is the smaller lengths' building-records, the centurial stones, that have survived and, although such evidence is lacking for the Antonine Wall (cf. *RIB* 2138, 2156, 2164), it appears that the method of allocation within the three legions may have approximated to the Hadrianic model (Fields 2003: 30–31).

From a study of the inscriptions on the distance slabs and from knowledge of their find spots, it has been estimated that the 37 miles (59.2km) of Wall-rampart were divided up into 15 building sectors. This total would allow easy sub-division among the three legions. There is clear evidence that attempts were made to keep the workload as even as possible, that is, the division of the rampart building into blocks of whole Roman miles or multiples of a third of a mile.

Table 3: Manpower for the Antonine Wall (after Hanson and Maxwell 1986: 132–36)

Unit	Work-party	No. of soldiers
legio II Augusta Caerleon (*Isca Silurum*)	75 per cent of full complement (based on distance slabs)	4,000
legio VI Victrix pia fidelis York (*Eboracum*)	Detachment only (based on size of labour camps)	1,500
legio XX Valeria Victrix Chester (*Deva Victrix*)	Detachment only (based on size of labour camps)	1,500
	Total manpower	**7,000**

Table 4: Building sectors for the Antonine Wall (after Hanson and Maxwell 1986: 121–31)

Sector	Distance (wall-miles)	Legion	Distance slab no.
Old Kilpatrick	four and two-thirds	*legio XX*	
Castlehill	three and two-thirds	*legio VI*	7, 8 (*RIB* 2194, 2196)
East Millichen	three and two-thirds	*legio II*	5, 6 (*RIB* 2186, 2193)
Cadder	two	*legio XX*	
East Cadder	two	*legio VI*	3 (*RIB* 2185)
Eastermains	three and two-thirds	*legio XX*	4 (*RIB* 2184)
Girnal Hill	two	*legio II*	
Dullatur	two	*legio XX*	19
Tollpark	three	*legio II*	
Dalnair	three	?*legio VI*	
Tamfourhill	three	*legio XX*	2 (*RIB* 2173)
?Langton	four	?*legio VI*	
Polmonthill	four and two-thirds	*legio II*	
Bridgeness	four and two-thirds	*legio XX*	1 (*RIB* 2139)

Building the Antonine Wall

Building the Antonine Wall

The construction of the Antonine Wall rampart is estimated to have used up a corridor of turf 50m wide to both front and rear of the frontier line, assuming that suitable turf was available nearby. The turf-work involved cutting turf blocks, loading them onto a man's back, transporting them, and unloading and placing them in position, most of which would have needed two men. Legionaries were unquestionably experienced in turf-work, as illustrated on Trajan's Column (scenes XI, XII, XXXIX, CXXVII), and one of the standard issues of the soldier's marching order was a crescent-shaped 'turf cutter'. Vegetius (3.8) describes a standard-sized building turf of 1.5 × 1.0 × 0.5 Roman feet (444 × 296 × 148mm).

This would have weighed about 30kg, though the weight is largely irrelevant as the load was determined not by weight but by size. Experimental work by the Royal Engineers at the Lunt, a first-century Roman fort near Baginton, Warwickshire, and pre-mechanisation military manuals and estimators' handbooks, all suggest a work-rate of around 10 minutes for cutting a single turf. Trajan's Column (scenes XX, LX, LXV) depicts turf carried on a legionary's back, secured with a rope sling, while the Lunt work showed that loading required two men and that turfs were relatively fragile. These were therefore probably lifted, carried, and placed as one operation. Two men were also likely for unloading and placing.

Over the 33 miles (52.8km) between Bridgeness and Castlehill the unit of measurement on the slabs was the Roman pace (*passus*), but over the 4 miles (6.4km) between Castlehill and the Clyde, Roman feet (*pedes*) were employed (there were 5 Roman feet in a pace). The reason for this change to a much shorter working length may be linked to the radical change in plan introduced while the Wall was still under construction, namely the decision to increase the number of forts along its line from six to 19. The Wall had been completed as far as Castlehill, when the legionary work-parties were diverted to the additional work of fort building. When this task was finished, they returned to complete the Wall, and, in order to speed the construction project up, the last four miles were divided into six short lengths, into which all the available legionary work-parties were concentrated. The decision to use the foot (*pes*) as the unit of measurement may derive simply from the shortness of the distance to be commemorated; the *pes* (0.2959m) was the normal Roman unit of measurement for distances of less than a mile.

On many of the distance slabs the inscribed panels are surrounded by carved figures representing legionary insignia, scenes of victorious battles, deities and cultic ceremonies. A prime example is the slab from Bridgeness (No. 1) on the east terminus of the Wall. The inscription (*RIB* 2139), with typical abbreviations, reads:

IMP(ERATORI) CAES(ARI) TITO AELIO / HADRI(ANO) ANTONINO / AVG(VSTO) PIO P(ATRI) P(ATRIAE) LEG(IO) II / AVG(VSTA) PER M(ILIA) P(ASSUUM) IIII DCL II / FEC(IT)

For the Emperor Caesar Titus Aelius Hadrianus Antoninus Augustus Pius, father of the country, *legio II Augusta* built [this work] for a distance of 4,652 paces

Shields called *peltae* flank the inscription. A sculptured panel on the left portrays an auxiliary trooper in a pose reminiscent of many cavalry tombstones as he, with spear poised to strike, tramples over four naked warriors. The relief panel on the right depicts a purification ritual known as a *souvetaurilia*, with a bull, sheep and pig being led to sacrifice at an altar. In this rare portrayal of the ceremony, while one priest plays a double flute, another pours a libation over the altar, probably devoted to the Roman war god Mars. Alternatively, the person officiating may be A. Claudius Charax from Pergamon in Asia Minor, the legate of *legio II*

The tombstone (*RIB* 2142) of Nectovelius, a Brigantian serving in *cohors II Thracum*, who died after nine years' service and was buried at Mumrills on the Antonine Wall. This is an unusual instance of an auxiliary soldier giving a place of origin as well as his unit. (Esther Carré)

43

Augusta in *c*. AD 143 (*RE* 1961.320). Whatever, the carved panels, like the Antonine Wall itself, conveyed a propaganda message that the combination of military might and divine favour made Rome irresistible.

Modern estimates, if indeed some 7,000 legionaries were involved in the building project and calculating that the number of productive hours in a working day is unlikely to exceed six, reckon the work could have been completed in 250 days or just over eight months. If the time available in any one year for building equalled that for campaigning, the Wall (excluding any forts) would have taken one and one-third seasons to complete.

The legionary work-parties were long enough at their construction work on the Antonine Wall to require living accommodation while so engaged. To date some 18 labour camps have been located by aerial survey along the line of the Wall, mainly to the south and within 400m of it.

Function

The new northern frontier system drew its strength from the occupation of a tactically dominant position. From east to west, wherever possible, it was drawn along the very crest of the escarpments and crags that run across the Forth–Clyde isthmus. Between Bridgeness and Falkirk it commands an area

Castle Greg fortlet, looking south-east from Camilty Hill (290m). Built by Agricola to monitor an east–west road that may have run along the northern flank of the Pentland Hills, the rectangular earth rampart survives as an impressive mould on all sides. Before afforestation of the surrounding area, the position occupied by the fortlet was one of bleak, open moorland. (Author's collection)

The double-ditch system and rampart mound of Castle Greg, looking north-west towards the fortlet's single entranceway. When originally dug, the V-shaped ditches would have been 3m deep. A split-timber or wattlework parapet, 1.5m high, crowned the earth rampart, while a timber tower stood over the gateway. (Author's collection)

Feature	Task	Man-days
Ditch	Removal of 955,000m³ soil at 3.8m³ per man per day	250,000
Rampart	1. Lay stone base 40,000m³ rough cobbles at 4.3m wide, 0.15m deep	60,000
	2. Construct turf superstructure 25–30 millions or 325–385 ha of turf, each block 0.5 × 1.5 × 1.0 Roman feet (Vegetius 3.8)	1,250,000
	3. Construct wooden breastwork 28,000 m³ of timber	60,000
Fortlets	1. Extra 2,460m of rampart	35,000
	2. Internal buildings	15,000
Military Way	Hand-in-hand with Wall-base	60,000
	Total man-days	**1,730,000**

Table 5: Man-days for the Antonine Wall (after Hanson and Maxwell 1986: table 6.7)

that in Roman times comprised salt marshes on the shores of the Forth and the low-lying flood plain of the River Carron. From Falkirk westward to the watershed near Kilsyth it looms above the ill-drained upper reaches of the Bonny Water (flowing into the Forth). It then, striding over the basalt massifs of Croy Hill and Bar Hill, descends the left bank of the Kelvin (flowing into the Clyde) as far as the outskirts of Glasgow. At Balmuildy it crosses the river, commits itself to a winding course across the southern outliers of the Kilpatrick Hills through Bearsden and the northern outskirts of Clydebank, and finally gains the right bank of the Clyde at Old Kilpatrick. Its total length was 37 miles (59.2km), roughly half that of Hadrian's Wall, but, despite its lesser dimensions and less permanent structure, it was by no means of inferior design, nor was it intended to serve as a temporary expedient.

It would be wrong of us to imagine vast hordes of the Caledonii hurling themselves at the Antonine Wall as the Roman defenders valiantly manned the rampart to oppose them. Even if the Wall had a protected walkway, the whole structure was not intended as a fighting-platform. It would have presented a determined enemy force with a difficult, but not impassable obstacle: the Wall was designed as a stumbling block rather than a barrier. Any such delays in crossing the Wall only gave the Romans more time to assemble a field force from its garrison and move to intercept the enemy. This was invariably the objective here as on the other frontiers, to bring the enemy to battle and defeat them swiftly and decisively. In most cases the mustering of a substantial tribal force should have been reported before it had a chance to make an attack. As on other frontiers, policing and diplomatic activity will have kept the northern tribes under observation. The outpost forts also had an important role to play here, allowing the army to monitor tribal activity well beyond the Wall.

Raiding, often on a very small scale, is likely to have been far more common than larger-scale attacks. The proximity of the empire would have opened up a lucrative market for the slave trade. Although slavery already existed among the indigenous communities the commercial aspects of the Roman slave trade may have encouraged an upsurge in raiding in the frontier zone. A legal text (*Digesta* 49.15.6, cf. 48.19.8) does refer to the case of a woman condemned to cook for convicts in a salt-works, but then captured from Roman northern Britannia in just such a foray. Carried across the frontier, she was subsequently sold back into the province and repurchased by her owner, a centurion named Cocceius Firmus, quite possibly the same centurion of *legio II Augusta* who set up the five altars (*RIB* 2174–78) at Auchendavy on the Antonine Wall (Birley 1953: 87–103).

Warlike tribal societies viewed small-scale military activity as a normal part of life, successful raids winning warriors plunder and giving them prestige amongst their own people. Where they were stronger than their neighbours, they did not need any greater provocation to attack them. As such, the Romans would have appeared no different from any other neighbours. If the Romans appeared to be weak – usually as a result of movements of troops from one frontier to a crisis

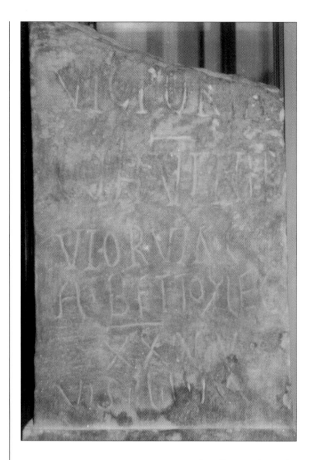

ABOVE LEFT An altar (*RIB* 2144) dedicated to Victory by *cohors VI Nerviorum*, from the *principia* of Rough Castle. The inscription imparts that Flavius Betto, a centurion who had been seconded from *legio XX Valeria Victrix* based at Chester, commanded this auxiliary unit. (Esther Carré)

ABOVE RIGHT The Roman road below Lead Law, to the north of West Linton village, looking north-east. The line of this road, which ran from Carlisle to the Forth, was later used as the basis for the turnpike from Edinburgh to Ayr, and more recently the line of the A702 has approximately followed it. (Author's collection)

elsewhere – then they would be raided. This weakness did not need to be actual, only perceived. Each successful raid added to this perception of their vulnerability, and so encouraged more frequent and larger raids. A small war-band crossing into the empire and rustling cattle or taking a few captives did not seriously challenge Rome's authority. Most raids did not penetrate very deep into the empire, which meant the frontier zone bore the brunt of the attacks. However, if this were allowed to happen frequently, then aggression against Rome would escalate. Unchecked, then this could lead to large-scale invasion.

In AD 196, when the governor, D. Clodius Albinus, became embroiled in an imperial power struggle with Septimius Severus, the Caledonii, for their part, were emboldened by the departure of the backbone of the garrison of Britannia to Gaul (Dio 75.4.1, Herodian 3.7.1–2). They joined with the Maeatae – which seems to have been a general name in use at the time for a confederation of tribes who lived near Hadrian's Wall – and the following year began to ravage the frontier zone. To keep the peace the new governor, Virius Lupus, paid the Caledonii and their allies off (Dio 75.5.4). Four hoards ending with the coins of Septimius Severus are known in Scotland, which suggests that the Romans 'purchased' peace on a number of occasions in this period through the payment of subsidies or bribes (it depends on one's point of view) to the northern tribes.

The Antonine Wall, as with the other frontier systems, helped to mark out Roman territory to any potential enemy, and the large impressive structures would confirm 'barbarian' impressions of the might of Rome and the glory of its empire. Frontier systems in particular helped the army to regulate movements and trade across the area, and made it difficult, if never impossible, for hostile groups to raid successfully. The roles of surveillance and supervision could obviously be more effectively discharged if the frontier system had a strong visual command of the territory in which it was to be set. The line selected for

A building inscription (*RIB* 2156) from Castlecary, Antonine Wall. This was set up by the *centuria* of Antonius Aratus, *cohors VI*, of an unspecified *legio*. It appears that construction work was allocated to individual centuries under the supervision of their respective centurions. (Esther Carré)

The rugged sculpture found by chance in the riverbed at Cramond in 1996. Some 1.5m long, it shows a recumbent lioness with prominent jagged teeth devouring a stylised, bearded man. Symbolising the destructive power of death, this stone carving probably once graced a military tomb outside the nearby fort. (Esther Carré)

the Wall, therefore, acquired the tactical domination of the terrain between the Forth and the Clyde. Likewise, the close spacing of the forts probably reflects a policy in favour of dispersal of troops along the Wall for police duties, as opposed to the concentration that would be desirable for major military operations.

The defences of these forts were relatively modest. This was not through lack of engineering skill, but a reflection of their function as barracks rather than strongholds. Roman military doctrine was to leave their defences and fight the enemy in the open whenever possible. If a fort was attacked, its simple ditches and ramparts were considerable obstacles as long as a sufficient number of defenders were present. Diplomatic activity and intelligence gathering monitored events beyond the frontier and ideally gave warning of future danger. Yet ultimately the security of the province rested more on Rome's reputation for military strength and this was best displayed when the army took the field. A frontier system was never intended to limit or restrict movements of the army, and always permitted punitive expeditions north of the Wall whenever it was considered necessary.

Garrison

The total garrison of the six primary forts would have been in the order of 4,000, including those manning fortlets. With the tripling of the number of forts along the Wall, the increase of the number of men was probably of the order of 75 per cent to around 7,000, which is almost exactly three-quarters of the garrison on Hadrian's Wall. In other words, expressed proportionally, the Antonine Wall had a garrison one and half times as strong as that on Hadrian's Wall, which, like Hadrian's Wall, consisted mainly of units of auxiliaries (*auxilia*).

Information about the units occupying these forts derives both from inscriptions and from their plans and layouts. The forts display a wide variety of sizes and internal plans. In theory the five largest – Mumrills, Castlecary, Bar Hill, Balmuildy, and Old Kilpatrick ranging from 3.2 to 6.5 acres (1.3–2.6 ha) in area – are designed to accommodate *cohortes quingenariae* at full strength. In practice, however, this may not have been the case. For example, unless transferred from Old Kilpatrick to Bar Hill, or vice versa, *cohors I Baetasiorum quingenaria* was permanently split between the two forts. Of the remainder, some may also have accommodated *cohortes quingenariae* – Cadder, Auchendavy, and Castlehill, for example – but the others are too small to have held anything but *vexillationes*. On Hadrian's Wall all known forts give the appearance of being on the linear barrier for convenience as well as each

Table 6: The probable garrisons of forts on the Antonine Wall

Fort Primary forts are in bold	Size acres / ha	Garrison Antonine I (c. AD 142–158)	Garrison Antonine II (c. AD 158–164)
Carriden coastal	4.0 / 1.6	*cohors quingenaria*	*cohors quingenaria*
Inveravon	?	?	?
Mumrills road north	6.5 / 2.6	*ala I Tungrorum quingenaria (RIB 2140)*	*cohors II Thracum quingenaria eq (RIB 2142)*
Falkirk	?	?	?
Rough Castle	1.0 / 0.4	*vexillatio* of unknown unit	*vexillatio of cohors VI Nerviorum quingenaria (RIB 2144-45)*
Castlecary road north	3.5 / 1.4	1. *vexillatio of cohors I fida Vardullorum milliaria eq cR (RIB 2149)* 2. *cohors I Batavorum quingenaria eq (RIB 2154)*	*vexillatio of cohors I Tungrorum milliaria (RIB 2155)*
Westerwood	2.0 / 0.8	*vexillatio* of unknown unit	*vexillatio* of unknown unit
Croy Hill	1.5 / 0.6	*vexillatio* of unknown unit	*vexillatio* of unknown unit
Bar Hill	3.2 / 1.3	*cohors I Hamiorum sagittaria quingenaria (RIB 2166–67, 2172)*	*vexillatio of cohors I Baetasiorum quingenaria cR (RIB 2169–70)*
Auchendavy	2.8 / 1.1	*cohors quingenaria*	*cohors quingenaria*
Kirkintilloch	?	?	?
Cadder	2.8 / 1.1	*cohors quingenaria peditata (cf. RIB 2187)*	*cohors quingenaria peditata*
Balmuildy river crossing	4.0 / 1.6	*vexillatio of cohors milliaria (cf. RIB 2189)*	*cohors quingenaria peditata or vexillatio of cohors quingenaria eq*
Bearsden	2.4 / 0.9	?	?
Castlehill	3.2 / 1.3	*vexillatio of cohors IIII Gallorum quingenaria eq (RIB 2195)*	?
Duntocher	0.5 / 0.2	*vexillatio* of unknown unit	*vexillatio* of unknown unit
Old Kilpatrick coastal	4.2 / 1.7	*cohors quingenaria eq or vexillatio of cohors milliaria*	*vexillatio of cohors I Baetasiorum quingenaria cR (RIB 2208a)*

Table 7: Legionary inscriptions from Antonine Wall forts (after Hanson and Maxwell 1986: table 8.3)

Fort	Building inscription	Altar	Tombstone
Castlecary	*centuria* of Antonius Aratus, *cohors VI*, unspecified *legio* (*RIB* 2156)	1. three by *legio VI Victrix pia fidelis* (*RIB* 2146, 2148, 2151) 2. one by *legio II Augusta* (*RIB* 2146) 3. one by unspecified *vexillatio* (*RIB* 2147)	
Westerwood		Vibia Pacata, wife of Flavius Verecundus, centurion of *legio VI Victrix pia fidelis* (*RIB* 2164a)[2]	
Croy Hill	three by *legio VI Victrix pia fidelis* (*RIB* 2161–63)	*legio VI Victrix pia fidelis* (*RIB* 2160)	three soldiers (father and two sons?) on a possible tombstone
Bar Hill	1. *legio II Augusta* (*RIB* 2171) 2. *legio XX Valeria Victrix* (*RIB* 2209)	*legio II Augusta* (*RIB* 2168)	
Auchendavy	*legio II Augusta* (*RIB* 2180)	five by M. Cocceius Firmus, centurion of *legio II Augusta* (*RIB* 2174-78)[2]	two soldiers of *legio II Augusta* (*RIB* 2179, 2181)
Cadder	*legio II Augusta* (*RIB* 2188)		
Balmuildy	two by *legio II Augusta* (*RIB* 2191–92)[1]		
Bearsden	*legio XX Valeria Victrix*		

Notes:
[1] Place the construction of the Wall in the governorship of Q. Lollius Urbicus (AD 139–143).
[2] Legionary centurions who may have commanded auxiliary garrisons, that is, seconded from their parent unit.

seemingly being designed for a complete unit (with one exception). Those on the Antonine Wall, on the other hand, are more closely integrated with the barrier while more flexibility also seems to have governed the disposition of the units, some forts being insufficiently large to hold the cohort attested there.

In addition, *vexillationes* of legionaries, from their bases at Isca Silurum (Caerleon), Deva Victrix (Chester) and Eboracum (York), seem to have formed or supplemented garrisons on the Antonine Wall. Inscriptions show that legionaries had not only constructed the Wall-forts but were also buried outside them, and that legionaries dedicated altars to favourite deities at several fort-sites.

There is definite proof too that legionaries from *legio XX Valeria Victrix* at least formed part of the garrison at one of the forts to the south of the Antonine Wall during the Antonine period. A series of inscribed altars (*RIB* 2122–25, cf. 2127) were erected by members of this legion at the fort of Newstead, which lay immediately above the crossing of the Tweed by Dere Street.

Success or failure?

Although both Strabo (4.5.3) in the first century and Appian (*praefatio* 5) in the second century tell us Britannia was not worth conquest economically, the Romans nevertheless occupied the island. The reason is given to us explicitly by Florus (*Epitome* 1.47.4), the poet-friend of Hadrian, who links Britannia to Armenia:

It was fine and glorious to have acquired them, not for any value, but for the great reputation they brought to the magnificence of the empire.

In practice, of course, this often meant bringing great reputation to a particular military governor, as Tacitus says (*Agricola* 27.1) his father-in-law Agricola knew.

Strife and glory go hand in hand. And strife on the northern frontier was endemic, judging from numerous, albeit vague, written references to wars and punitive campaigns throughout the first and second centuries. Nevertheless,

The fort at Bar Hill

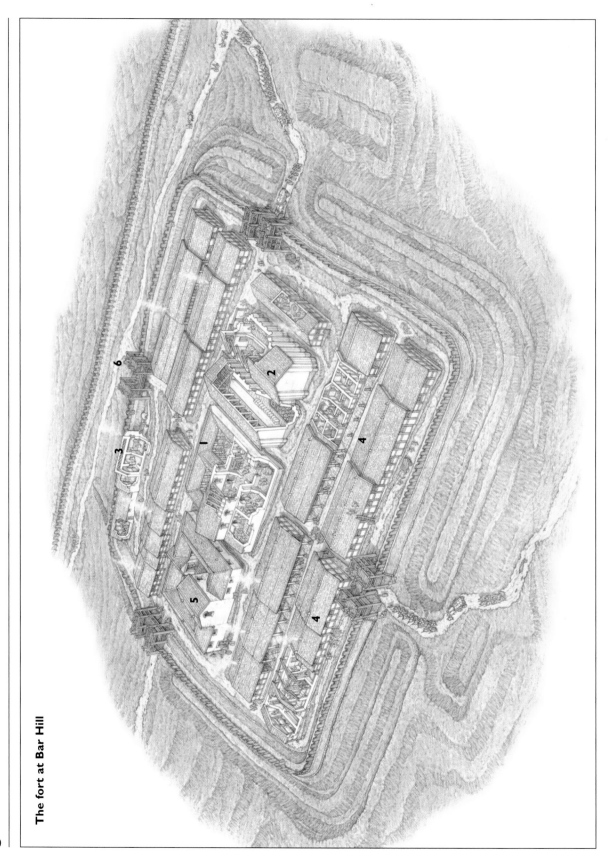

The fort at Bar Hill

The fort at Bar Hill, the highest (150m) on the line of the Antonine Wall, covered an area of about 3.2 acres (c. 1.3 ha). A rampart of turf resting on a stone base some 3.7m in width, which was defended by a double ditch-system except on the north side where there was a single ditch, enclosed the fort. It was not set directly against the Wall itself – the latter passed by about halfway down on the north flank of Bar Hill while the fort sat squarely on the summit, thereby gaining superb views northwards to the Campsie Fells across the upper valley of the River Kelvin. The Military Way passed between the fort and the Wall. Inscriptions (*RIB* 2166–67, 2169–70, and 2172) indicate that the fort was garrisoned by *cohors I Hamiorum*, a specialist archer unit from Syria, and later by *cohors I Baetasiorum*, a unit originally recruited from the Baetasii tribe inhabiting the lands between the Rhine and the Meuse. Comprehensive excavations between 1902 and 1905 (re-excavated 1978–82) showed that the fort contained a headquarters building (**1**, *principia*), a pair of granaries (**2**, *horrea*) and an intramural bathhouse (**3**, *balneum*) complete with attached communal latrine, all stone-built, and timber-framed barrack-blocks (**4**, *centuriae*). There should also have been a residence (**5**, *praetorium*) for the garrison commander. In this reconstruction the *praetorium* is to the left of the centrally placed *principia*, to the right the *horrea*, to the north and south lie the *centuriae*. The stone-built bathhouse lies just inside the north rampart, between the north gateway (**6**) and the north-west corner of the fort.

The view north-west from Bar Hill fort with the slopes of the Campsie Fells rising on the north side of the Kelvin valley. The watery strip of the Forth & Clyde Canal follows the alignment of the Antonine Wall westward. For the garrison the superb views north and west would not have been obstructed by the trees. (Author's collection)

northern Britannia was for the Romans very much of a peripheral importance, to be annexed if political expediency supported an expansion of the province, and to be quickly abandoned when troops were needed elsewhere. By the time the Antonine Wall was built the Romans had some awareness that there were areas beyond an empire essentially centred on the Mediterranean basin, which could bring them little economic advantage and were best left to the 'barbarians'. As the Greek Appian, who was an imperial official under Antoninus Pius, states (*praefatio* 7):

> The Romans have aimed to preserve their empire by the exercise of prudence rather than to extend their sway indefinitely over poverty-stricken and profitless tribes of barbarians.

Some limits were perfectly logical. Despite the importance of glory in conquest, there was also the necessity of making the enterprise worthwhile economically. From the Mediterranean viewpoint Britannia was remote and mysterious, and here we see in Appian something of the conscious decision making in Rome. In other words, emperors were mindful of what we would call the marginal costs of imperialism. As a former *advocatus fisci* (financial secretary to the emperor), Appian had sound knowledge of the cost of empire building. In discussing Britannia, he says (*praefatio* 5):

> They have occupied the better and greater part of it but they do not care for the rest. For even the part they do occupy is not very profitable to them.

Castlelaw hillfort, Pentland Hills, looking south-west from Castle Knowe (331m). On its east side, built into the inner ditch, is a 20m-long earth-house (*souterrain*) for the bulk storage of grain. Finds of Roman artefacts, mainly glass, indicate the probable destination of the grain. It is not entirely coincidental that its construction coincides with the Antonine advance into Scotland. (Author's collection)

The left-hand panel of the Bridgeness distance slab (No.1), showing an auxiliary trooper riding down four naked warriors. The motif of the triumphant horseman is commonplace on Romano-British cavalry tombstones. (National Museums of Scotland)

In recent years there have been major advances in our knowledge of ancient settlement and agriculture around the area of the northern frontier. For instance, an ecological study (Greene 1986: 124–27, fig. 52) of the region of north-eastern England to the north and south of Hadrian's Wall has provided good evidence that the proportion of grassland was higher to the north and that of cereal land greater to the south. It appears, therefore, that there was a desire to maximise the area of arable land within the frontier zone.

After the advances and withdrawals between the occupation of Hadrian's Wall and the Antonine Wall, the Forth–Clyde line was finally abandoned in the reign of Marcus Aurelius. But later Septimius Severus launched a new campaign in the footsteps of Agricola with the explicit aim, according to his contemporary Herodian (3.14.2), to win glory and victories in Britannia. And so the personal character of imperial foreign policy produced eccentric (*vide* Mann 1979, Whittaker 1994), not scientific (*vide* Luttwak 1976, Ferrill 1991), decisions. Thus the extension of the empire was not a smooth progress, but 'go, stop, go'. The Romans, although they had strategic notions, were incapable of forging the complicated interrelationships of grand strategy. Their world was substantially a world without maps, and their view of geography was simplistic and crude, making detailed planning extremely difficult. Besides, it was in the nature and makeup of the Roman worldview to conquer and dominate. As Isaac rightly emphasises, the Romans 'conquered peoples, not land' (1992: 395).

So a combination of factors prompted the successive withdrawals. The resistance and hostility to the army of occupation, especially from the Caledonii, was to be set beside the difficult terrain and harsh climate and in general the pointlessness of further expenditures of men and *matériel* to secure progressively poorer land, with little obvious economic return. Britannia was always a fringe province of the empire. It is in this context that the Antonine Wall and the annexation of lowland Scotland needs to be viewed.

Case study 5: anatomy of an Antonine fort

The best preserved of the Antonine Wall forts, Rough Castle was home of *cohors VI Nerviorum*, an auxiliary unit originally raised among the Nervii of Gallia Belgica, a tribe that had come very close to defeating C. Iulius Caesar at the battle of Sambre (Scheldt), 57 BC (*Bellum Gallicum* 2.23–27). The designation

'Nervii' itself was Celtic, meaning 'people of Nerios', Nerios being a Celtic god whose name meant 'the strong one'. According to Caesar (*Bellum Gallicum* 2.4.7), the Nervii were reputedly the fiercest of all the Belgae. The unit is first attested in Britannia in AD 122 when it came over from Germania Inferior with the new governor, A. Platorius Nepos (*CIL* 16.65). Although the Antonine Wall was built in AD 142/143, the cohort was not transferred to Rough Castle until the second occupation period (*c.* AD 158–164), as is confirmed by a building inscription (*RIB* 2145) and an altar (*RIB* 2144) dedicated to Victory, both from the headquarters building (*principia*).

The latter inscription also imparts that Flavius Betto commanded the unit, a centurion seconded from *legio XX Valeria Victrix* based at Deva Victrix (Chester). The appointment of legionary centurions to the command of auxiliary units was not uncommon, although the officer in charge was customarily a prefect (*praefectus cohortis*), a Roman citizen of equestrian rank serving in the first step of the *tres militiae*, the threefold military service requirement of all who entered upon public life. However, when a suitable candidate for the prefecture could not be found among the equestrians, the post might be filled by the secondment of a relatively senior centurion from a legion.

Abutting the south face of the Wall-rampart, this fort was relatively small, extending to 1 acre (0.4 ha) in size and was enclosed, on its other three sides, within a double ditch-system and earth ramparts. Gateways, flanked by wooden gate-towers, were located on each of its four sides, with causeways across the defensive ditches to allow access. The Military Way passed through the fort as its *via principalis*. A fortified annex, twice the size of the fort itself, was added later to the east, and contained a stone-built bathhouse, for use by the garrison, as well as timber-framed buildings of uncertain character. The fort itself included some substantial stone buildings in the central range, the *principia*, the *praetorium* and a single *horreum* for the storage of grain, particularly spelt and bread wheat, and other perishable foodstuffs.

As the fort sits upon a flat plateau, the visitor is afforded a splendid view of the profile of the Wall-ditch and Wall-rampart against the western skyline. One of the main attractions of the site, however, must be the system of 10 rows of oblong pits, which once contained sharpened stakes camouflaged by twigs and foliage, that lie just beyond the Wall to the north-west of the fort. Such pits have been detected on the berm in front of the Wall at various points (e.g. Falkirk, Croy Hill). According to C. Iulius Caesar (*Bellum Gallium* 7.73, cf. *Frontinus Strategemata* 1.5.5), his soldiers fondly referred to these pitfalls as *lilia* (literally 'lilies'). Identical 'pottis', 'with stykkis and with gres all grene' (John Barbour *The Brus* 11.379), were employed by Robert Bruce to hinder English cavalry at Bannockburn (1314). Simple booby-traps such as these have been employed in more recent conflicts, most notably the 'pungi sticks' used by the Viet Minh and their famous descendants, the Viet Cong.

Legionaries on Trajan's Column are regularly shown exhibiting their field-engineering skills. An analogy for the construction work on the Antonine Wall, this scene (Scene XI) depicts a work-party cutting, transporting and laying turf blocks, in addition to excavating a ditch. (Reproduced from Lepper, F. and Frere, S.S. *Trajan's Column: A New Edition of the Cichorius Plates*, Sutton, Stroud, 1988)

Case study 6: Nectovelius, *miles* of Brigantia

A mid-second-century tombstone from Mumrills, the largest fort on the Antonine Wall, bears the following inscription (*RIB* 2142):

DIS M(ANIBVS) NECTOVELIVS F(ILIVS) / VINDICIS AN(NORVM) IXXX / STIP(ENDIORVM) VIIII NAT / IONIS BRIGANS / MILITAVIT IN / COH(ORS) II THR(ACVM)

[To the spirits of the departed Nectovelius, son of Vindex, aged 29, of 9 years service, a Brigantian by tribe, served in *cohors II Thracum*]

The supply-depot at Cramond

This reconstruction illustrates the supply-depot at Cramond during the Severan period. Although not on the Antonine Wall itself, the coastal fort at Cramond was an integral part of the frontier system. Situated on the southern shore of the Firth of Forth, the large fort, some 5.7 acres (c. 2.3 ha), was built around AD 142 and shares the same history as the Wall. The *principia* (**1**) is located at the centre of the fort, surrounded by *centuriae* (**2**) and *fabricae* (**7**). The site also contains an extramural bathhouse (**3**) and *vicus* (**6**). Positioned conveniently where the River Almond (**4**) flows into the Forth (**5**), the fort's associated harbour facilities provided a good anchorage for transport ships, and Cramond probably served as the key supply-depot for the Wall. It was thoroughly repaired and reorganised at the beginning of the third century, when it was used as a base for Septimius Severus' northern campaigns. Evidence (*RIB* 2134) suggests that part of *cohors V Gallorum quingenaria equitata* was stationed here until it was returned to South Shields in AD 222 (cf. *RIB* 1060).

This auxiliary unit was part-mounted (*equitata*) and contained a nominal 500 men (*quingenaria*) originally recruited from amongst the various tribes of Thrace, who inhabited the area between the Aegean Sea and the Black Sea.

The deceased (note the latinised form of his name) belonged, however, to the nation of Brigantes, a confederacy of tribes in northern Britannia. In pre-Roman times, the Brigantes, which Tacitus (*Agricola* 17.1) describes as the most numerous of all the Britannic tribes, had probably been at daggers drawn with most of the tribes of southern Scotland, and more recently had apparently shown considerable animosity to the occupying army. Yet Nectovelius died in the service of one, presumably as a *miles cohortis* as rank is not stated, protecting the other. This tombstone is one of the few sources available that refer to Britons serving in the Roman army, but, as in other frontier provinces, by the second century many recruits in auxiliary units were of local origin. Harnessing local people was a shrewd policy and we should never, therefore, automatically assume that members of auxiliary units had any connection with nominal homelands.

Most ordinary soldiers were recruited in their late teens or early to mid 20s and enlisted for 25 years, with a reward of citizenship on honourable discharge (*honesta missio*) from the army. Nectovelius had signed up aged 20 or thereabouts, but he was to die after only nine years' service. A study of mortality in the empire suggests that, up to retirement, soldiers, despite their profession, had a greater life expectancy than civilians did. Upon retirement the position was reversed and civilians fared better. The food and medical care given to soldiers and their active lives must have played a large part in securing their welfare. Military tombstones rarely record how the man died, and how Nectovelius came to die so young, whether by disease, as is most likely, or as a result of enemy action, we can never know.

During excavations over the years at Mumrills fort a number of animal bones have been uncovered, including those of ox, sheep, pig, red deer and wolf – the latter animal very likely being hunted and killed for sport and as a means of pest control. The meat was either boiled in bronze camp-kettles, or roasted on spits. Likewise, chicken, to provide both meat and eggs, made due contribution to the daily fare. Shellfish, as evidenced by the great abundance of oyster and whelk shells, also augmented the soldiers' diet. Being stationed close to the Forth, the garrison at Mumrills obviously took the opportunity to obtain shellfish. The implicit testimony of numerous amphora fragments on the site indicates the consumption of *acetum* (sour wine), which is supplemented more explicitly by the Greek graffito GLYK[YS OINOS], ('sweet wine'), on an amphora shard (*RIB* 2493.14). Another example exhibits handwriting giving the actual production date of the contents. Distinguishing marks like this were presumably intended to indicate vessels containing vintage wine (*vinum*) as opposed to sour. Other archaeological finds included ceramic cheese-squeezers, showing that the garrison at Mumrills manufactured its own cheeses from the milk of domesticated animals.

Even such comparatively simple tombstones as Nectovelius' were costly items. One of the deductions from a soldier's pay was a standard contribution to the burial-club organised by the standard-bearer of the soldier's century

The supply-depot at Cramond

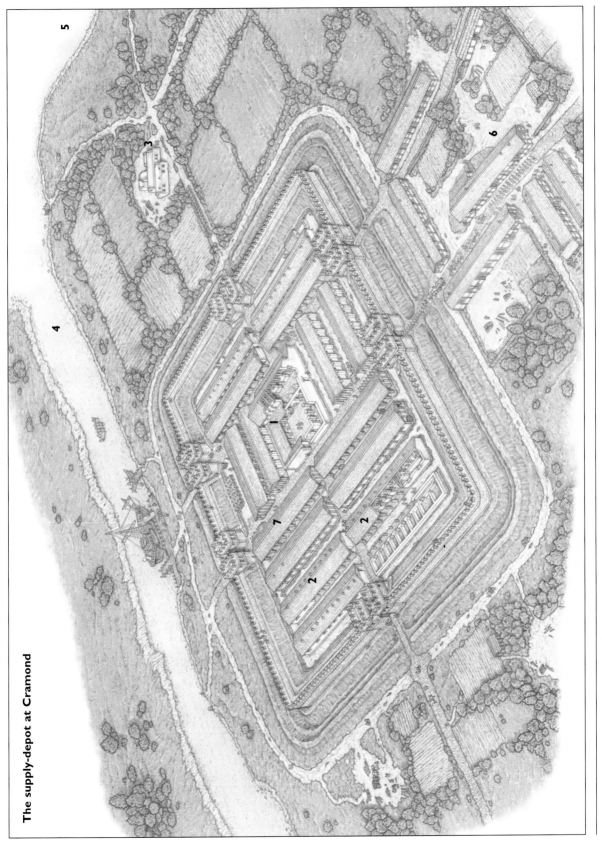

Table 8: The Antonine Wall – success or failure?

1 Occupation	
Antonine I	c. AD 142–158
Antonine II	c. AD 158–164
Severan	AD 208–211 (Mumrills, Croy Hill, Cadder, Old Kilpatrick)
	c. AD 222 (*RIB* 2134, *cohors V Gallorum eq* at Cramond)

2 Aims
a) To repel assaults upon the frontier zone from the north, that is, to act as a safety-valve or regulator.
b) To serve as a base for military operations beyond the frontier zone.
c) To foster the growth of 'romanisation' of Roman-protected territory without check or hindrance.
d) To control population movement and monitor taxes, tolls and trade within the frontier zone.

3 Imperial politics		
Vespasian Titus Domitian	AD 77–84	1. 'Conquest' of the far north by Cn. Iulius Agricola 2. Agricola recalled by Domitian: Tacitus bitterly comments that 'Britannia was conquered and immediately abandoned' (*Historiae* 1.2, cf. *Agricola* 10.1)
Domitian	AD 82	1. Detachments (*vexillationes*) from nine legions, including all four stationed in Britannia, serving under a *primus pilus* in the war against the Chatti (*ILS* 9200) 2. Likewise, a separate *vexillatio* from *legio VIIII Hispana* was present under its *tribunus laticlavius* (*ILS* 1025, cf. Tacitus *Agricola* 26.1)
	AD 86	1. Inchtuthil, the newly built fortress on the Tay, decommissioned 2. *legio II Adiutrix pia fidelis* redrawn for service on the Danube – one of its centurions, T. Cominius Severus, decorated in the Dacian war of AD 89 (*ILS* 9193) – and thus garrison of Britannia cut from four to three legions
Trajan	c. AD 105	1. A *vexillatio Britannica* is recorded at the legionary fortress of Noviomagus (Nijmegen) on the lower Rhine 2. The line of forts along the Stanegate marks the northern limit of military occupation in Britannia
Hadrian	AD 122	1. Visit of Hadrian to Britannia (*SHA* Hadrian 11.2) and arrival of new governor, A. Platorius Nepos (*CIL* 16.69) 2. Construction of Hadrian's Wall started during governorship of Platorius Nepos (*RIB* 1051, 1427, 1634, 1637–38, 1666, 1935 cf. *SHA* Hadrian 11.2)
Antoninus Pius	AD 139–142	1. Arrival of new governor, Q. Lollius Urbicus (*RIB* 1147) 2. Advance into lowland Scotland (*SHA* Antoninus Pius 5.4, cf. Pausanias 8.43.4)
	AD 142–143	1. Antoninus Pius hailed as *imperator* (*CIL* 10.515, *RIC* Antoninus Pius 743–45) 2. Construction of Antonine Wall during governorship of Lollius Urbicus (*RIB* 1147, *SHA* Antoninus Pius 5.4)
	c. AD 158	1. Reinforcements for three legions of Britannia from the garrisons of Germania Superior and Inferior under a new governor, Cn. Iulius Verus (*RIB* 1322) 2. Abandonment of Antonine Wall during governorship of Iulius Verus (*RIB* 283, 2110)
	c. AD 158	Reoccupation of Antonine Wall during governorship of Iulius Verus (*EE* 9.1383, cf. *RIB* 1132)
Marcus Aurelius	c. AD 164	1. Reoccupation of Hadrian's Wall during governorship of Sex. Calpurnius Agricola (*RIB* 1137, 1149, 1703, 1809) 2. Chatti invade Germania Superior and Raetia, while Parthians seize Armenia and defeat two Roman armies (*SHA* Marcus Antoninus 8.7, 22.1) 3. Returning troops from Parthian campaign bring *pestis Antoniniana*, which ravaged much of the western-half of the empire (Ammianus Marcellinus 23.6.24, cf. *SHA* Lucius Verus 8.1–2)
Septimius Severus	AD 208–210	1. Campaigns against the Caledonii (Herodian 3.14.2–10, 15.1-3, Dio 76.13) 2. Coin issue (*RIC* Septimius Severus 332) celebrating the emperor's victory in Britannia (VICTORIA BRIT.)
Caracalla	AD 211	1. Septimius Severus dies at Eboracum (York), and Caracalla becomes emperor (Herodian 3.15.2, 4, Dio 76.15.2) 2. Abandons his father's northern conquests and returns to Rome (Herodian 3.15.6–7, Dio 77.1.1)

4 Northern Tribes		
Domitian	AD 82–83	Takes two campaigning seasons for Agricola to bring Caledonii to defeat at Mons Graupius (Tacitus *Agricola* 25–38)
Trajan	c. AD 105	Battle honour *Ulpia Traiana* awarded to *cohors I Cugernorum*, along with a block grant of *civium Romanorum*, that is, Roman citizenship to all of its serving men (*RIB* 2401.6, *CIL* 16.69, cf. 48)
Hadrian	c. AD 118	1. Fronto says (*De Bello Parthico* 2) many soldiers killed by Britons 2. 'Britons could not be kept under control' (*SHA* Hadrian 5.2)
	AD 119	1. 'the barbarians had been scattered and the province of Britannia recovered' (*RIB* 1051) 2. Coin issue (*BMC* III Hadrian 1723) depicting personification of Britannia in a 'dejected' pose 3. T. Pontius Sabinus, erstwhile *primus pilus* of *legio III Augusta pia fidelis*, decorated by the deified Trajan on the '*expeditone Brittanica*' (*ILS* 2726B, cf. 2735) 4. C. Iulius Karus, prefect of *cohors II Asturum*, decorated '*bello Brittanico*' (*AE* 1951.88)
Antoninus Pius	AD 139–142	Lollius Urbicus 'overcame the Britons' (*SHA* Antoninus Pius 5.4, cf. Pausanius 8.43.4)
Marcus Aurelius	AD 161	War was 'threatening in Britannia' (*SHA* Marcus Antoninus 8.7)
	AD 170–172	Threat of another '*bellum Britannicum*' (*SHA* Marcus Antoninus 22.1)
	AD 175	5,500 Sarmatian cavalry despatched to Britannia (Dio 71.16.2)
Commodus	AD 180	1. Britons penetrated 'the wall' and 'did great damage and cut down a commander and his troops' (Dio 73.8.2) 2. Halton Chesters, Rudchester and Corbridge destruction deposits
Septimius Severus	AD 197	To keep peace, Caledonii paid a large sum of money by the governor, Virius Lupus (Dio 75.5.4)
	AD 208	'The barbarians of the province were in a state of rebellion' (Herodian 3.14.1)
	AD 208–210	1. The emperor takes the title Britannicus, 'conqueror of Britannia' (*SHA* Severus 18.2, *ILS* 431) 2. *legio VI Victrix pia fidelis* awarded an added title Britannia (*RIB* 2460.71–75)
	AD 210	Caledonii rise in 'rebellion' (Dio 77.15.1-2)
Severus Alexander	c. AD 230	Falkirk hoard, containing some 2,000 silver *denarii*, suggests Rome 'purchased' peace again through the payment of subsidies
5 Geography		
Lowlands	1. 'Tame' agricultural landscape 2 Resources such as grain, stock, timber, coal and slaves 3. Supply of recruits for auxiliary units of the Roman army	
Highland massif	1. Barren mountains rising to 1,000m, with a few over 1,300m 2. Lacking in mineral deposits and arable land	
6 Socio-political		
Exploit cultural barrier between Brittonic people and (relatively backward) proto-Pictish people	1. Flavian 'glen-blocker' forts 2. Flavian forts, fortlets and watchtowers	1. Highland Line 2. Ardoch-Strageath-Bertha axis (Gask Ridge '*limes*')
'See and be seen'	Antonine outpost forts	Strathallan-Strathearn-Tay axis
Full-scale expedition	1. Severan supply-depot 2. Severan base for legions	1. South shore of Forth (Cramond) 2. South shore of Tay (Carpow)
Imperial prestige	AD 43	Claudius decides 'Britannia was the place where a legitimate triumph could be most readily earned' (Suetonius *Divus Claudius* 17.1)
	AD 77–84	Agricola is a 'lover of glory' (*militaris gloriae cupido*, Tacitus *Agricola* 5.3)
	AD 139–142	Antoninus Pius seeks personal glory (*CIL* 10.515, *RIC* Antoninus Pius 743–45)
	AD 208–210	1. Septimius Severus is a 'lover of glory' (Herodian 3.14.2) 2. Dio indicates (77.13.1) that Septimius Severus intended to subjugate the whole of Britannia

(Vegetius 2.22, cf. Onasander 36.1–2). Should he die during service, this would then cover the cost of a basic funeral. It is doubtful, however, that the burial-club paid for more than the most rudimentary of markers for the grave, but like Nectovelius many soldiers had set aside money to pay for expensive stone monuments. The amount paid annually to rank-and-file auxiliaries during Augustus' reign was 750 *sestertii*, while during that of Domitian it had risen to 1,000 *sestertii* or 250 *denarii* (Campbell 24), sums that amounted to about five-sixths of a legionary *stipendium*. Before Domitian, wages were paid in three annual installments. His pay-rise perhaps added a fourth installment (Campbell 21). The first payment was made on the occasion of the annual New Year parade when the troops renewed their oath to the emperor. Official deductions were made for food and fodder. In addition, each soldier had to pay for his own clothing, equipment and weapons (Campbell 24, 25, cf. Tacitus *Annales* 1.17), but these items were purchased back by the army from the soldier or his heir when he retired or died. These were the official charges.

Severus Alexander (r. AD 222–235) is said to have had the motto: 'One need not fear a soldier, if he is properly clothed, fully armed, has a stout pair of boots, a full belly, and something in his money-belt' (*SHA* Severus Alexander 52.3). Unsurprisingly, therefore, the Roman army seems to have been most attractive as a career to the poorer sections of society. For such men, the *auxilia* offered a roof over their head, food in their bellies, and income in coin. Overall a soldier's life was more secure than that of an itinerant labourer. Naturally, we must remember the harsher side of such a career. It came at the price of 25 years of service. During that time a soldier not only ran the risk of being killed or crippled by battle or disease, but also, on an everyday basis, was subject to the army's brutal discipline.

ABOVE A close-up of one of the *lilia* at Rough Castle, the pen giving some idea of scale. In the bottom of the pitfall smooth stakes were set, hardened in the fire and with sharpened ends. The pitfall was then third-filled with earth, the rest of the space being covered with twigs and foliage to conceal the trap. (Author's collection)

RIGHT Legionaries constructing an earth-and-timber fort, as shown on Trajan's Column (Scene LXV). Here we see legionaries working in pairs, one placing a turf block onto the other's back, with the load being secured with a rope sling. (Reproduced from Lepper, F. and Frere, S.S. *Trajan's Column: A New Edition of the Cichorius Plates*, Sutton, Stroud, 1988)

The sites today

South of the Antonine Wall the fort at Birrens (nearby is the Roman artillery range at Brunswark Hill), near the village of Middlebie, is worth visiting. At Newstead, a village on the east fringe of Melrose, the flattened-out platform where the fort once stood and faint trace of the ditch hollows is still visible. Newstead lies in the shadow of the Eildons, which gave the name Trimontium (literally 'Triple Mountain') to the Roman fort, and the Iron Age hillfort, the largest in Scotland, on Eildon Hill North (404m) was a major centre of the local Selgovae. This fortified site contains some 300 circular house-platforms, representing the homes of a population of between 1,000 and 2,000 people. But such intense occupation did not continue as the Romans erected a watchtower on the western extremity of the summit. The shallow ditch that enclosed the watchtower can still be seen today.

Much of the Antonine Wall lies in the urban belt that runs between Edinburgh and Glasgow. Nevertheless, there are interesting remains to be seen at Callendar Park and Watling Lodge (ditch), both in Falkirk, Rough Castle (ditch, rampart, fort earthworks, annexe) and Seabegs Wood (ditch, rampart, Military Way), both outside Bonnybridge, Bar Hill (fort buildings), near Twechar, and Bearsden (bathhouse, latrine-block), a northern suburb of Glasgow. Additionally, at the latter location, the stone base for the rampart is visible in Hillfoot Cemetery. All these locations are easily accessible by car. For the more energetic, the six miles from Castlecary to Twechar, over Croy Hill and Bar Hill, forms a good walk with the Wall-ditch visible for most of the route (follow signposts for 'The Antonine Way'). All these monuments are accessible to the public and are in the care of Historic Scotland.

North of the Antonine Wall the earthwork remains of the fort at Ardoch are spectacular. Located just outside the village of Braco, the five crisp V-shaped ditches of this fort still survive in an astonishing state of preservation on both its north and east sides. Although Inchtuthil has slight remains, there is sufficient to convey the great size of a legionary fortress. Part of the military road that runs along the spine of the Gask Ridge can still be traced, and several watchtowers and the fortlet, one of the best preserved in Scotland, at Kaims Castle are still visible above ground. Of the watchtowers, those most worth visiting are at Parkneuk, Kirkhill and Muir o' Fauld. The line of the road can be followed on foot from Ardunie farm to Midgate.

The Museum of Scotland, part of the National Museums of Scotland in Edinburgh, holds the core of the material from the 1905–10 excavations at Newstead, as well as material from Birrens, Fendoch and the Antonine Wall. The Hunterian Museum, University of Glasgow, has the bulk of the material from the Antonine Wall, including all but one of the distance slabs.

Useful contact information

Historic Scotland

Tel.	(+44) 131 668 8600
Fax	(+44) 131 668 8669
Email	hs.ancientmonuments@scotland.gsi.gov.uk

National Museums of Scotland		**Hunterian Museum**	
Tel.	(+44) 131 247 4422	Tel.	(+44) 141 330 4221
Fax	(+44) 131 220 4819	Fax	(+44) 141 330 3617
Email	info@nms.ac.uk	Email	hunter@museum.gla.ac.uk

Bibliography

Armit, I., 1997, 2000. *Celtic Scotland*. London: Batsford/Historic Scotland.

Bidwell, P., 1997, 2002. *Roman Forts in Britain*. London: Batsford/English Heritage.

Birley, A. R., 1973. 'Petillius Cerealis and his conquest of Brigantia'. *Britannia* 4: 179–90.

Birley, A. R., 1976. 'The date of Mons Graupius'. *Liverpool Classical Monthly* 1.2: 11–14.

Birley, E., 1953. *Roman Britain and the Roman Army: Collected Papers*. Kendal: Titus Wilson.

Breeze, A., 2002. 'Philology on Tacitus' Graupian Hill and Trucculan Harbour'. *Proceedings of the Society of Antiquaries of Scotland* 132: 305–11.

Breeze, D.J., 1993. *The Northern Frontiers of Roman Britain*. London: Batsford.

Breeze, D.J., 1996, 2000. *Roman Scotland: Frontier Country*. London: Batsford/Historic Scotland.

Breeze, D.J. and Dobson, B., 2000. *Hadrian's Wall*, 4th edition. London: Penguin.

Ferrill, A.L., 1991. *Roman Imperial Grand Strategy*. Lanham: University Press of America.

Fields, N., 2003. *Hadrian's Wall, AD 122–410*. Oxford: Osprey (Fortress 2).

Gillam, J.P., 1975. 'Possible changes in the plan in the course of the construction of the Antonine Wall'. *Scottish Archaeological Forum* 7: 51–56.

Greene, K., 1986, 1990. *The Archaeology of the Roman Economy*. London: Batsford.

Hanson, W.S., 1987, 1991. *Agricola and the Conquest of the North*. London: Batsford.

Hanson, W.S. and Maxwell, G.S., 1986. *Rome's North West Frontier: The Antonine Wall*. Edinburgh: Edinburgh University Press.

Henderson, A.A.R., 1985. 'Agricola in Caledonia: the sixth and seventh campaigns'. *Classical Views* 29: 318–35.

Holmes, N., 2003. *Excavation of Roman Sites at Cramond, Edinburgh*. Edinburgh: Society of Antiquaries Scotland (Monograph 23).

Isaac, B.H., 1992. *The Limits of Empire: the Roman Army in the East*, 2nd edition. Oxford: Clarendon Press.

Keppie, L.J.F., 1979. *Roman Distance Slabs from the Antonine Wall: A Brief Guide*. Glasgow: Hunterian Museum.

Keppie, L.J.F., 1980. 'Mons Graupius: the search for a battlefield'. *Scottish Archaeological Forum* 12: 79–88.

Keppie, L.J.F., 1985. 'Excavations at the Roman Fort of Bar Hill, 1978-82'. *Glasgow Archaeological Journal* 12: 49–81.

Keppie, L.J.F., 1998. *Scotland's Roman Remains*, 2nd edition. Edinburgh: John Donald.

Lepper, F.A. and Frere, S.S., 1988. *Trajan's Column: A New Edition of the Cichorius Plates*. Gloucester: Sutton.

Macdonald, G., 1934. *The Roman Wall in Scotland*, 2nd edition. Oxford: Clarendon Press.

Mann, J.C. (ed.), 1969. *The Northern Frontier in Britain from Hadrian to Honorius: Literary and Epigraphic Sources*. Newcastle upon Tyne: Museum of Antiquities.

Mann, J.C., 1979. 'Power, force and the frontiers of the empire'. *Journal of Roman Studies* 69: 175–83.

Maxwell, G.S., 1989. *The Romans in Scotland*. Edinburgh: Mercat Press.

Maxwell, G.S., 1989. *A Battle Lost: Romans and Caledonians at Mons Graupius*. Edinburgh: Edinburgh University Press.

Maxwell, G.S., 1998. *A Gathering of Eagles: Scenes from Roman Scotland*. Edinburgh: Canongate Books/Historic Scotland.

Rainbird, J.S., 1969. 'Tactics at Mons Graupius'. *Classical Review* 19: 11–12.

Richmond, I.A. (ed.), 1958. *Roman and Native in North Britain*. Edinburgh: Nelson.

Robertson, A.S., 2001 (revised and edited by L.J.F. Keppie). *The Antonine Wall: A Handbook to the Surviving Remains*. Glasgow: Glasgow Archaeological Society.

Shirley, E.A.M., 2001. *Building a Roman Legionary Fortress*. Stroud: Tempus.

Shotter, D.C.A., 1996. *The Roman Frontier in Britain: Hadrian's Wall, the Antonine Wall and Roman Policy in the North*. Preston: Carnegie.

St Joseph, J.K.S., 1978. 'The camp at Durno, Aberdeenshire and the site of Mons Graupius'. *Britannia* 9: 271–87.

Woolliscroft, D.J., 2002. *The Roman Frontier on the Gask Ridge, Perth and Kinross*. Oxford: BAR British Series 335.

Whittaker, C.R., 1994, 1997. *Frontiers of the Roman Empire: A Social and Economic Study*. Baltimore: John Hopkins University Press.

Abbreviations

BELOW LEFT Legionaries constructing a military road, as shown on Trajan's Column (Scene XXIII). Here two legionaries are ramming home the metalling. Invariably, this surface was made up of small stones, flints or gravel, as opposed to cobblestones. (Reproduced from Lepper, F. and Frere, S.S. *Trajan's Column: A New Edition of the Cichorius Plates*, Sutton, Stroud, 1988)

BELOW RIGHT An earth-and-timber watchtower on the Danube, as depicted on Trajan's Column (Scene I_5). Coupled with the archaeological data, such scenes provide the basis for reconstructing the watchtowers that lined the military road across the Gask Ridge. (Reproduced from Lepper, F. and Frere, S.S. *Trajan's Column: A New Edition of the Cichorius Plates*, Sutton, Stroud, 1988)

Glossary

The following provides much of the terminology associated with Roman fortifications of the first and second centuries and their garrisons. In most cases both singular and plural forms are given (i.e. singular/plural).

acetum Sour wine

acta diurna Daily-orders

agger/aggeris
1. Rampart
2. Raised bed of a road

ala/alae Cavalry 'wing'

annona Rations

aquilifer Bearer of a legion's eagle-standard (aquila)

armilla/armillae Armlets – military decoration

as/asses Copper coin (= ¼ sestertius)

ascensus Stairway

aureus Gold coin (= 25 denarii)

ballistarium/ballistaria Platform for stone-thrower (ballista) or bolt-thrower (catapulta)

balneum/balneae Bathhouse

beneficiarius/beneficiarii Senior officer's aid

bipennis/bipenna Double-edged axe

buccellata Hardtack

bucinator/bucinatores Musician who blew the bucina, a horn used to regulate watches

burgus/burgi Watchtower

caespes Turf

campus Parade-ground

canabae Extramural settlement (fortress)

capitus Fodder

capsarius/capsarii 'Para-medic'

cena Evening meal

centuria/centuriae
1. Cohort sub-unit
2. Barrack-block

centurio/centuriones Centuria or legionary cohort commander

cervesa Celtic beer

cervus/cervi Chevaux-de-frise

clava/clavae Wooden practice-sword

clavicula/claviculae Curved extension of rampart protecting a gateway

clibanus/clibani Bread-oven

cohors peditata/cohortes peditatae
1. Auxiliary cohort. cohors quingenaria peditata: 480 infantry (6 centuriae) under a praefectus cohortisc. cohors milliaria peditata: 800 infantry (10 centuriae) under a tribunus.
2. Legionary cohort, 10 per legion. cohors prima: 800 legionaries (5 'double-strength' centuriae) under a primus pilus. cohortes II–X: each 480 legionaries (6 centuriae) under a pilus prior.

cohors equitata/cohortes equitatae Mixed auxiliary cohort of foot and horse

contubernium/contubernia Mess-unit of eight infantry, 10 per century

cornicen/cornicines Musician who blew the cornu, a horn associated with the standards

cornicularius/corniculari Junior officer responsible for clerks in principia

corniculum/corniculi Horn-shaped military decoration – awarded for bravery

corona/coranae Crown – military decoration generally reserved for centurions and above

corona absidionalis crown of grass – awarded for rescuing besieged army

corona aurea gold crown – awarded for various exploits

corona civica crown of oak leaves – awarded for saving life of a citizen

corona muralis mural crown in gold – awarded to first man over walls of besieged town

corona vallaris rampart crown in gold – awarded to first man over enemy's rampart

cratis/cratisis Wickerwork practice-shield

cuneus/cunei 'Wedge', i.e. irregular cavalry unit

curator/curatoris Turma second-in-command

custos armorum Armourer

decurio/decuriones Turma commander

denarius/denarii Silver coin (= 4 sestertii)

deposita Soldiers' bank

diploma/diplomata Military discharge certificate

dolabra/dolabrae Pickaxe

dona militaria Military decorations

duplicarius Soldier receiving double-pay

dupondius/dupondii Brass coin (= 2 asses)

emeritus/emeriti Veteran

eques/equites Trooper

excubitor/excubitores Sentinel

explorator/exploratores Scout

fabrica/fabricae Workshop

fossa/fossae Ditch

frumentarius/frumentarii Intelligence officer

frumentum Wheat

honesta missio	Honourable discharge
hordeum	Barley
horreum/horrea	Granary
imaginifer	Bearer of the emperor's image (*imago*)
immunis/immunes	Soldier exempt from fatigues
intervallum	Open space between rear of rampart and built-up area
latera praetorii	Central part of fort between *viae principalis* and *quintana*
lavatrina	Latrine-block
legatus Augusti legionis	Legio commander (senatorial rank)
legio/ legiones	Legion (5,120 men all ranks)
libra	Roman pound (= c. 323g)
librarius/librarii	Clerk
librarius horreorum	kept granary records
librarius depositorum	collected soldiers' savings
librarius caducorum	secured belongings of those killed in action
lilia	Pits containing sharpened stakes (*cippi*)
lorica	Breastwork
ludus	Amphitheatre
medicus/medici	Medical orderly
medicus ordinarius/medici ordinarii	Doctor
mensor/mensores	Surveyor
miles/militis	Soldier
mille passus/milia passuum	'One-thousand paces' (Roman mile = 1,618 yards/1.48km)
milliaria/milliariae	'One-thousand strong'
missio causaria	Medical discharge
missio ignominiosa	Dishonourable discharge
modius/modii	Unit-measure (= 8.62 litres)
murus caespiticius	Turf wall
numerus/numeri	'Number', i.e. irregular infantry unit
optio/optiones	*Centuria* second-in-command
pala/palae	Spade
palus/pali	Post for practising swordplay
papilio/papiliones	Tent
panis militaris	Army bread
passus/passuum	'One-pace' (5 Roman feet = 4 ft 10½ inches/1.48m)
patera/paterae	Mess-tin
pedes/peditis	Infantryman
pereginus/peregini	Non-Roman citizen
pes/pedis	Roman foot (= 11½ inches/29.59 cm)
phalera/phalerae	Disc – military decoration
pila muralia	Palisade stakes – double-pointed with central 'handgrip' to facilitate lashing
praefectus castrorum legionis	*Legio* third-in-command responsible for logistics
praetentura	Forward part of fort from *via principalis* to front gate (*porta praetoria*)
praetorium	Commander's quarters
prandium	Lunch
principales	Three subordinate officers of a *centuria* (*optio, signifer, tesserarius*)
principia	Headquarters
prosecutio	Escort duty
quingenaria/quingenariae	'Five-hundred strong'
retentura	Rear part of fort from *via quintana* to rear gate (*porta decumana*)
rutrum/rutri	Shovel
sacramentum	Oath of loyalty
sagittarius/sagittarii	Archer
sesquiplicarius	1. *Turma* third-in-command 2. Soldier receiving pay-and-a-half
sestertius/sestertii	Brass coin (= ¼ *denarius*)
sextarius/sextarii	Unit-measure (= 1/16 *modius*)
signaculum/signaculi	Identity disc ('dog tag')
signifer	Bearer of a standard of a centuria or turma – responsible for unit's finances
signum/signi	1. Standard 2. Watchword
stabulum/stabuli	Stable-block
stipendium	Pay
tabularium/tabularii	Record-office
tessera/tessarae	Plaque bearing password
tesserarius/tesserarii	*Centuria* third-in-command – responsible for sentries and work-parties
tiro/tironis	Recruit
titulus/tituli	Short mound with ditch forward of a gateway
torque/torques	Neckband – military decorations
tres militiae	Equestrian career-structure (*praefectus cohortis* 'tribunus angusticlavius' *praefectus alae*)
tribunus/tribuni	One of six senior officers, after the *legatus*, of a *legio*
tribunus militum legionis laticlavius	second-in-command (senatorial rank)
tribuni militum angusticlavii	five in total (equestrian rank)
tubicen/tubicenes	Musician who blew the *tuba*, a trumpet used to signal commander's orders
turma/turmae	*Ala* sub-unit
turris/turres	Tower
vallum	Palisade
valetudinarium/valetudinaria	Hospital
vexillarius/vexillarii	Bearer of a *vexillum*
vexillatio/vexillationes	Detachment
vexillum	Standard of a *vexillatio*
via praetoria	Road leading from *principia* to *porta praetoria*
via principalis	Principle road extending across width of fort, from *porta principalis dextra* to *porta principalis sinistra*
via quintana	Secondary road parallel to *via principalis*
via sagularis	Perimeter road around *intervallum*
vicus/vici	Extramural settlement (fort)
vinum/vini	Wine, usually vintage
vitis	Centurion's twisted-vine stick

Index